T

# THE FLESH

## and the

# FRUIT

Remembering Eve and the Power
of Creative Transgression

# Vanya Leilani

WOMANCRAFT PUBLISHING

*Published by Womancraft Publishing, 2024*
*womancraftpublishing.com*

*ISBN 978-1-910559-96-3*
*The Flesh and the Fruit is also available in ebook format:*
*ISBN 978-1-910559-95-6*

*Cover image © Natalia Berlik*

*Womancraft Publishing is committed to sharing powerful new women's voices, through a collaborative publishing process. We are proud to midwife this work, however the story, the experiences and the words are the author's alone. A percentage of Womancraft Publishing profits are invested back into the environment reforesting the tropics (via TreeSisters) and forward into the community.*

*A percentage of royalties from this book supports the reforestation projects of TreeSisters (treesisters.org)*

# PRAISE

*If, after reading this book, your life hasn't changed and you don't feel renewed and awakened, read it again, more slowly.*

**from the Foreword by Thomas Moore, New York Times bestselling author of *Care of the Soul***

*I have not been as electrified by a book since* Women Who Run with the Wolves. *Vanya's sensuous unpacking of the Eden myth intricately braids together the personal, symbolic and cultural to reveal new depths in this foundational story and its ongoing shadow over the feminine psyche. She masterfully shows how the tired trope of Eve's temptation has wrongly vilified feminine power and creativity for millennia. This meticulous skewering of toxic interpretations puts forth a refreshing, soulful vision of Eve finally reclaimed as a heroine of consciousness and sovereignty.*

The Flesh and the Fruit *had me choked up as Vanya articulates with piercing clarity so much of what I've felt but struggled to name about the dangers of prioritizing obedience over ingenuity. She exposes the rotten core at the heart of paradigms that promise women safety through smallness. This book shattered tired myths in my own mind and - despite the seeming darkness of our age - awakened a thrilling sense of transgressive possibility. Layered with poetic memoir, cultural commentary and sacred feminine scholarship,* The Flesh and the Fruit *points the way toward finally revisioning Eve as she should be honored, not as humanity's downfall, but as our liberation.*

**Lisbeth Cheever-Gessaman, artist and illustrator of *The Divine Feminine Oracle***

*What if we conceived of Eve as powerful, creative, curious? Not fallen, but wildly transgressive and able to choose her own path in life. In her excavation of the Eden myth, the author skilfully reimagines this foundational story that has stained women as sinful and shameful. In doing so, she liberates us to discover a way back to our truest and most alive Selves.*

**Mary Reynolds Thompson, author of *The Way of the Wild Soul Woman* and *Reclaiming the Wild Soul***

*Dr Vanya Leilani explores the Eden myth as a foundation stone of patriarchy and domination. She weaves together her own lived experiences growing up in a conservative Christian community with her deep understanding of psychology and myth to show us how profound and invasive the story of the woman to blame is in our western culture. If we are, as I believe, the stories we have been told and tell ourselves, then this book reveals Eve as the mother of us all.*

*A beautiful blend of scholarship and a life well-lived,* The Flesh and the Fruit *can be a light held up to show the way toward true sovereignty and freedom.*

**Gina Martin, High Priestess, author of the** *When She Wakes* **and** *Daughters of the Goddess* **series**

The Flesh and the Fruit *is an important addition to feminist literature. Dr. Vanya Leilani engages with the immediacy of this moment in time through rich, detailed research into mythologies and the lyricism of her own story. The reader is invited into conversation with common cultural narratives that shape how we see ourselves and the world. Her insights and wisdom illuminate the path for women in search of a more sovereign way. This book is a must-read for anyone who has transgressed (or longs to) only to find a richer world on the other side. If you are interested in a subversive read of the mythologies that shape, inhibit and ultimately offer to set us free, read this gorgeous and magical book.*

**Natalie Bryant, author of** *Muddy Mysticism: The Sacred Tethers of Body, Earth and Everyday*

The Flesh and the Fruit *weaves memoir and mythology through one woman's profound journey to claim her sovereignty and her whole and holy self. Bittersweet and so very relatable to women seeking the sacred in their own image,* The Flesh and the Fruit *is an important addition to the growing collection of women's work that invites and inspires us to look within our deepest knowing to find the answers to the questions that Patriarchy doesn't want us to ask. Both fierce and tender, it provides steady companionship for women at every stage of their individual and spiritual rebirth.*

**Amy Wilding, author of** *Wild & Wise: Sacred Feminine Meditations for Women's Circles and Personal Awakening*

# CONTENTS

*For Ash,*
*I love you.*

# FOREWORD

If, after reading this book, your life hasn't changed and you don't feel renewed and awakened, read it again, more slowly. This a beautiful book on the life of the soul, and it is full of insights that could shift your perspective on many things central in your life. I appreciate how it is so intelligent and yet written in a way that is 'down to earth.' Not just practical or easy to read, but also bubbling up from the depths. It is not distant but is intimate in every way and at every step.

Vanya evokes Eve. You know that she has met this mythic woman and tells us what she has seen, not just what she knows. This Eve turns out to be very different from what you have heard from theologians and preachers. She is a goddess whose transgression, heeding the wily serpent and eating the juicy fruit of life, offers all of us what we need to enjoy and fulfill our natures. Eve is not just one of a number of interesting mythic figures. In Vanya's skillful presentation of her she is truly the mother of all mothers, and, as you are thinking about her, her myth becomes the very meaning of life. It is far richer than anything you may have been imagining when you first opened the book.

Seamlessly, Vanya moves from mythology to personal history to a bit of theory, grounding all of her brilliant insights in daily life. It's fascinating to me to imagine that the figure of Eve offers so much to an understanding of life and a remarkable path to dealing with many of its mysteries.

My own idea of transgression focuses on Eros, the god the ancient Greeks called "world-maker," who is also the potency we feel in desire, connection and pleasure. We associate eros with sex, and it's true that sexuality is one way that erotic life manifests. You could expand your idea of sex and arrive at eros. But my point is that eros always asks you to transgress. Sex and eros both have an extra spice when a transgression is involved.

I often tell the story of my father's one-hundredth birthday. After the party was over, I pushed him in his wheelchair to his room in the nursing home. On the way we passed a bowl of bananas, and he signaled me to go that way. He grabbed two or three and stuffed them under his blanket. Then he looked at me with a smile, "They don't let me have these."

At that moment I knew that my father's erotic life was in good shape, which meant that his soul was awake and at work. He could enjoy a simple transgression that hurt no one. Besides, this was the father I knew, someone who never liked to obey unnecessary and punishing rules. Without being able to articulate it, he honored Eve all his life.

Vanya calls this "creative transgression," a means for keeping life renewed and fresh, always rising to the surface. She describes how Eve took the forbidden fruit and ate it as the juices dripped down her arm. Transgression is often in the service of a more sensuous life, because that is the kind of experience apparently feared by patriarchal masters of the universe.

Thinking of Eve and my father, naturally I also think of my mother, because Eve, we know, is the mother of us all. Some have tried to convince us that she is a bad mother because she caused us to lose Paradise. But Vanya corrects that wrong impression. My mother followed all the rules of her church religiously, but she was a true mystic, and she transgressed easily when her heart opened in compassion.

I am happy to see that Vanya has a sure understanding of Archetypal Psychology, an approach developed by my friends James Hillman, Patricia Berry and Rafael Lopez-Pedraza. It's the only one that makes complete sense to me but is quite subtle and therefore not well-known. Vanya makes this psychology, too, down to earth, and is skillful in applying it to daily life.

After reading this book you may want to get a statue of Eve to put next to Venus, Asklepios, Jesus, the Buddha and other favorite saints—these are mine. I think I'll place her next to Hermes, the tricky god of clever language, who brings dreams and guides souls. After Vanya's stellar work on her mythology, Eve belongs in a place of honor and veneration. We could all benefit from having her bold, colorful spirit deep in our hearts.

**Thomas Moore, New York Times bestselling author of *Care of the Soul***

# PROLOGUE

*We have tried to put ourselves into the forms of the world,*
*but we are not contained there, beautiful even as they are.*
*We constantly spill over the borderlines and boundaries.*

**Beverly Lanzetta**[1]

My God died on a Tuesday. He had been ailing for quite some time. If I had not loved him so much, maybe I would have noticed the wheezing, the raspy whispers of warning. If I had not been such a good girl, I may have noticed I was sick with his illness: that I, too, was dying. I was just sitting on a cheap lawn chair in a dorm room meeting with other resident assistants. On the surface life drummed on, but I felt the moment of his death like an inner earthquake—the ground opened up beneath me and swallowed me whole. And like Persephone, I fell into the underworld.

I grew up hearing and believing that God had died to save me; that my salvation depended upon the sacrifice of a god, that nothing else could wipe away my shame. As it turns out, the death of my God did save me. My God was ill and so I was ill, and because he died, I was freed to find my life.

On that Tuesday evening the fragile thread that had been holding me together was severed by an invisible faithful hand, and my world fell apart, the pieces falling like seeds scattering in the wind. The barely contained questions that had been quietly sprouting in my thirsty heart broke out of their hidden greenhouses and grew like vines, binding my body, leaving me exhausted and unable to continue as I was.

I became the ghost of my dead God's last breath. That God took me with him to his grave. I would be reborn many years later— knowing not of gods but of mysteries, devoted not to answers but to questions, shaped by curiosity rather than judgment. I would be reborn from the ashes of that dead God knowing that *I had never been bad and that I would never again be good.*

I would be knowing.

I would be sovereign over my own life.

I would be like Eve.

At the boundaries between the approved life and the knowing life, Eve has found me over and over again. I have sat, quiet in the moment of her transgression. Deep in the cells of my body, in the hidden silences between inhale and exhale, I have felt the power of desire that is stronger than fear and tasted the sweetness of a wild longing that is stronger than obedience. Desperately, I have searched for her courage in the dark pregnant emptiness between worlds—my arms stretched between them, my own crucifixion. With trembling hands, I have reached for freedom, for nourishment, for beauty, for knowing.

My childhood was tightly woven together with the threads of the Christian tradition. I learned about Adam and Eve at a young age. I have no memory of *not* knowing that Woman caused the fall of creation from divine favor, and that because of her, we were all born sinful and guilty. I had always been aware that because of Eve's transgression, I could not trust my body, heart, or mind, I could never trust my desire or longing. I had always known that because of her the Earth was damned. We were all cursed. Because Eve was the first to sin and second to be created, women would always take second place and could never lead, but instead should serve and be silent.

While I knew the myth well in childhood, it was in my adult life that I recognized the archetypal Eve, that is, the psychospiritual force she brings and represents. In my early twenties as I wandered off the preset path, I began to discern the archetypal Eve woven through the way I experienced the world: Eve not as a literal woman but as a way of being, as a style of consciousness, as a constellation of experiences. As I wrestled with the deep disorientation created by the act of leaving the prescribed life, the conflict and guilt of betrayed loyalties, and the intoxication of a strange admixture of doubt and courage, a dear friend reminded me that we were, in that moment, "daughters of Eve." I began to notice Eve as a psychological and spiritual experience that comforted me and terrified me. This Eve was not the literalized Eve that has for so long been a stand in for every (fallen and guilty) Woman and served as justification for horrific social injustices. The Eve I encountered was the mythic and archetypal Eve that shows us something about our deep lives.

The Eve I know now is radically different from the Eve of my childhood. But, one thing about her has remained true: Eve is dangerous.

Eve is dangerous because she does transgress; she does step beyond prescribed boundaries into unknown territory; she does cause worlds to fall apart. Eve is dangerous because she chooses knowing over goodness and sovereignty over safety. She disobeys in order to answer the call of her heart and body. She is guided by her longing.

Once I began to really know this Eve, I understood that she is homeopathic: she has carried our illness and she has also carried our medicine. All these years, Eve has been here with us, waiting to show us the way out of the Garden into the wildness of our own voices. Eve now rises from the safety of the prescribed life, from the prison of a too-small paradise, from the shadowed places of her exile, and reminds us of a commandment we have too often forgotten: *Thou shalt transgress.*

This book weaves the Eden myth, collective cultural narratives, and my own personal stories into a braided portrait of the power of creative transgression toward the creation of new consciousness. To transgress means *to step beyond or across*. Creative transgression is the act of stepping across pre-assigned boundaries, beyond obedience to the status quo, and creating something new.

With this book, I hope to bring to awareness the stories that keep us obedient to paradigms that promise safety and favor in exchange for our knowing and sovereignty. To be sovereign is to be self-governing, to stand at the center of our own circles, and to live out of the inner law of our own nature. This work involves naming the places of constrictive obedience, challenging the internal and cultural narratives that turn us against our nature, tending injured instinct so we might live with more freedom and more truth, and cultivating ways of being and knowing that enable us to stand at the center of our own circles.

Creative transgression into new life calls for a return to our wildness as powerful source of permission, blessing, and knowing. This book is meant as a siren song calling us home as we walk out of the 'shoulds' and the too-small spaces in our lives and into our own wild nature, into our wild knowing.

# THE EDEN STORY

*We cannot understand the history of Eve
without seeing her as a deposed Creator-Goddess.*

**John Phillips**[2]

Once upon a time there was a Garden.[3]

It was full of light, and where there is light there is shadow.

The Keeper of the Garden created it from a wasteland. The Keeper made the skies and the seas and the land and filled them all with all kinds of plants and creatures. He called it good.

But the Keeper wanted more. So, he sculpted the dust of the land into a form he called Man. Once the clay figure was shaped, the Keeper awakened Clay Man with his breath. And all was well.

However, in time, the Keeper noticed Clay Man was lonely. So, together they searched far and wide for a suitable companion, but none was found. The Keeper entranced Clay Man into a deep sleep and removed one of his crooked bones, and from that bone shaped and breathed life into Bone Woman. Finally, Clay Man had a companion.

The Keeper of the Garden told them about their lives in this Garden. They could eat from the bounty of the land and all the fruit of the trees…except from the tree in the center of the Garden. It was called the Tree of the Knowledge of Good and Evil. *From this tree never eat,* the Keeper warned them. *If you do, you will surely die.* Clay Man and Bone Woman eagerly agreed to obey this command.

For a time, they enjoyed their lives in the peaceful Garden and were protected and watched over by the Keeper. They often walked in the cool of the evening in the safety of the Garden with rivers running through.

Bone Woman obeyed and served and enjoyed the favor of both the Keeper and Clay Man, but slowly a small pearl of discontent began glowing in her hidden and growing heart. The pearl was not named but made itself evident when one evening, Bone Woman heard the voice of the serpent, and this time, she listened.

The serpent, a most cunning creature, knew something Clay Man and Bone Woman did not know because their eyes were closed to the shadows of the Garden—they could not see all that was hidden in the depths of things. They could only see the surface, the overt. The serpent, an ancient carrier of wisdom and the oldest companion to the goddesses, spoke to Bone Woman.

*Listen,* the serpent said, *if you eat of the fruit of the Tree of the Knowledge of Good and Evil you will not die. Instead, you will become like the gods.*

Bone Woman stood and heard these words. Her obedient mind urged her to keep walking and to turn away, but her body vibrated with curiosity and the glowing pearl suddenly felt like a fire in her chest. Still, she said no.

The serpent persisted and again told Bone Woman she would certainly not die. She would become like the gods.

Something in her was stronger than obedience, stronger than fear, and she looked at the fruit while Clay Man waited by her side. As she stood still in front of what had been forbidden, she saw something surprising: the fruit was beautiful. She saw that it is good for food. She saw that it is good for knowing. Standing there in front of what had promised certain death, she saw only beauty, nourishment, pleasure, and knowing.

Finally, the pearl of discontent broke open in her body and became longing. She felt her desire for beauty, nourishment, pleasure, and knowing and from her awakened desire she reached out her trembling hand, plucked the ripe fruit from the tree and brought it to her hungry mouth. She took a bite of its flesh and the fluid ran down her chin and neck. Clay Man, witnessing all of this, also took the fruit into his body.

In an act of deep communion with the wild magic of the tree, the flesh of the fruit became one with the flesh of their bodies, and their eyes were opened. Now they could see everything, even what lived in the shadows.

They saw they were naked.

They realized their being-ness.

They were awakened to their autonomy.

They covered their bodies with leaves from the tree.

Later, when they heard the Keeper walking through the Garden, they were afraid. They felt ashamed of what had changed in them. The seeing and the knowing felt forbidden and they hid. But the Keeper found them and saw that they had changed—that their eyes had been opened. They could see themselves now. And they could see the Keeper now.

The Keeper, realizing their transgression and transformation, covered their bodies and pronounced curses over them all. Curses for reaching for the forbidden fruit and for choosing beauty, nourishment, pleasure, and knowing over obedience and safety.

Cursed Serpent made to crawl on its belly and to be forever crushed by Woman's heel.

Cursed Woman to live in subjugation to Man and to pain in childbirth.

Cursed Land to be dominated and conquered by Man.

Cursed Man to be at war with the land in relentless toil and labor.

After the curses had been delivered, Clay Man named Bone Woman *The Mother of All the Living.*

The Keeper, once he pronounced his curses, gathered the other Keepers. They were afraid. They knew the serpent's words were true—that taking of the flesh and the fluid of the fruit of the Tree of Knowledge would not kill Clay Man and Bone Woman; it had made them like the gods.

*Yes, now they have become like us,* they confirmed in council. *Now they are knowing. What if they eat from the Tree of Life and live forever?* And so, for their knowing, they were exiled.

The Keepers were so concerned that they decided Clay Man and Bone Woman should be cast out of the Garden lest they continue their transgressions and become immortal like the gods. They sent them out to the Land of Nod, the land of wandering. They placed guardians around the Garden to ensure that the Tree of Life would be kept safe from mortals thereafter.

Bone Woman was named Eve.

Clay Man was named Adam.

Thereafter, both were named fallen and guilty.

Thereafter, Eve became Everywoman, cursed into an inferior and denigrated place.

Until one day, what was buried in the story was unburied.

Until one day, the Goddess in the Garden was seen again.

Until the seeds planted in the Garden broke open.

And so it happened, that one day the One Who Forgot became the One Who Remembers. She had been taught that she must remain obedient because she was a daughter of Eve. And she obeyed. Until her own pearl of discontent began to hum below the surface of her life, and her longing became stronger than her fear.

She remembered that Eve meant *Lifegiver*. Suddenly, the hushed rivers of her grandmother's whispers baptized her memory, uncovering what was buried there. She remembered a Goddess: Asherah the *Lifegiver*. She remembered an ancient line of Earth Mother goddesses, that like Eve, were called the *Mother of all the Living*.

She remembered the grandmothers gathered in circles speaking of a time when they would go to the sacred tree in high places to worship the Goddess—the tree a symbol of her divinity, knowledge, wisdom, oracular knowing, enlightenment, and revelation. *Lady of the Sycamore*, they whispered sometimes in their prayers.

Her grandmother used to speak of the serpent that had guarded the tree for thousands of years. Sometimes the Goddess herself was a serpent. Calling the Goddess *Serpent Lady* was another way of naming and honoring the cyclical death and rebirth, self-regeneration, and divination through the Goddess.

The One Who Remembers felt the longing she had seen in her grandmother's eyes as she told stories of worshipers sitting in sacred circles passing around a branch heavy with ripened fruit. Each worshipper would take a bite from the fruit, taking in the flesh and the fluid of the Goddess. In this way, even as the juices ran down their chins and necks, they knew some of the power of the Goddess had been shared with them.

How could she have forgotten these stories, the stories of her grandmothers? They had almost been erased. Almost.

On this day, her eyes were opened. The One Who Remembers saw the Eden story in a new way. She understood the sacred tree and the serpent as the Goddess herself. She understood Eve's humiliation as the exile of the Goddess to whom her grandmother whispered her worship and love. She understood that below the surface of the story of Eve's exile, the story of the dethronement of the Goddess was written in invisible ink. Buried in the story was everything she could not yet know but would need to remember when the time came.

The story was a seed.

On this day of remembrance, she saw Eve's instinct as she walked the Garden. She felt the pull of Eve's obedience as she listened to the serpent's true words. She felt the deep wrestling as Eve lived between what she was told to believe and what she saw and felt with her own body. She felt the hunger Eve felt when she saw that the fruit was beautiful and good for knowing and nourishment. As she perceived the wild story planted in the Garden, she felt her hands tremble with Eve's as she reached for the forbidden fruit and she tasted the sweet fruit in her mouth. She realized that what was used to humiliate Eve—the serpent, the tree, and the fruit—were the Goddess setting her free.

It was as if The One Who Remembers fell into a trance where she saw the Sky Father gods gathering in council after Eve reached for and ate the fruit. They were worried and agitated. She heard them cry, *Now they have become like us, knowing! What if they eat from the tree of life and live forever?*

These words wove themselves around her and remade her world.

The serpent was telling the truth. Eve had become like the gods. Her eyes had been opened and now she saw, and she knew.

She was not cast out because of her depravity and sin. She was cast out because of her wild knowing, because of her sovereignty.

The One Who Remembers now knew what was planted in the shadows of the Garden: a way out of obedience into sovereignty. And on that day, she set out in search of her own transgressions out of the Garden of obedience into sovereignty.

# BOOK ONE:
# SEEDS PLANTED IN
# THE SHADOWS

*To understand why the Eden story is so important we have to remember the extraordinary way origin myths operate in our psyches. In a way humans are not made of skin and bone as much as we're made of stories. The Eden myth perhaps more than any other floats in our cells, informing our vision of ourselves and the world.*

**Sue Monk Kidd**[4]

# BURIALS & SEEDS

*New seed is faithful. It roots deepest in the places that
are most empty...I am certain that in every fallow
place, new life is waiting to be born anew.*

**Clarissa Pinkola Estés**[5]

I grew up in an intentional religious community in southeastern
rural Brazil – in a brick house on the top of a small hill. The house
was nestled in a cluster of big buildings that held a community of
Christian missionaries. Each morning at 5:30 am, someone would
run down to the bottom of the hill and ring the bell—that is, they
would pick up a small, rusty pipe and swiftly strike a bigger pipe that
hung from an old wooden post. It was a ritual of waking to seek God
before the sun rose, a communal rolling out of bed in the dark into
communion with something greater.

From my room at the top of the hill, I would begin to hear singing,
praying, crying, and laughing as hundreds of seekers found secret
places for reaching out to God. *It was magical.* I loved the messy
cacophony of humanity and divinity in those sounds that rolled up
the hill, past the banana leaves, and into my little pink room.

In many ways this setting suited my naturally contemplative nature
very well. It gave me a way of being in this world, while also being in
the unseen worlds. I loved living a devotional life. My small child's heart
basked in the sense of purpose and meaning. Most of all, I loved these
images that filled me with a sense of wonder, a sense of connection to
something unnamable, a sense of the world's unseen spiritual depths.

But these treasures came with instructions written in stone.

The stones were heavy and cast long shadows.

Even as I devoted my life to an unfathomable mystery, I did it from a too-small space. The purpose and meaning were singular and narrow. The One Way was etched in everything we said and did and aspired to. The One Way offered a certain safety, and also unyielding walls. Walls are notable in that they simultaneously keep things out and in. This is how what keeps us safe might also become our prison.

I was once visited by a dream that taught me about burial, about cunning. It showed me something about courage and about the secret of seeds. In the dream, I was around twelve years old and my very best friend, my closest companion, was a large beautiful Polar Bear. We roamed the land where I grew up, always together. But the village feared Bear. And one day, down the hill from my childhood home, at the entrance to an area we called *os fundus*, "the depths," the community cornered us with torches and pitchforks. They were afraid and they would attack and conquer Bear. I was frantic with fear and desperation. With arms outstretched, I placed my body between the people and Bear. "He is not dangerous. He is my friend!" I screamed and cried. Until Bear, also so afraid, stood up on his hind feet and, towering over us, he roared a terrifying roar. I looked up at him and, suddenly, I was also afraid of Bear. I ran up the hill to my house and from the living room window, I watched the community attack Bear, my truest and closest friend. I wept, feeling helpless and ashamed. As he rolled in the mud on the ground he was being slowly hidden as his white fur turned into the color of Earth. "Play dead," I whispered as I watched him disappear. "Play dead," I prayed as I wept. I knew that playing dead, hidden in the mud of the Earth, was the only way Bear would survive. "Play dead. Play dead. Play dead!" Now, years after this dream visited me, I know that Bear—what was most precious, knowing, and true in me—did not die. Bear only waited, like a seed buried deep in my own heart for a time when it would be safe to thrive. Sometimes what is most true and most precious in us turns to seed, buried in the dark, not because of weakness but because of a deep faithfulness to our own survival, because of an ancient crone knowing that shows us how to be held safely until we can be reborn into the world.

When I was born, I was handed many instructional stone tablets that told me who I was: female firstborn, the daughter of a spiritual leader, a servant consecrated to the Christian God before birth. Later, I would be visited by many dreams of church services where I was named the holy sacrifice.

Everything that was not written on those tablets was made into seeds and buried until the time was right. They waited in the dark for the moment of creative transgression out of what had held them and into the light. Bear had to play dead, covered in mud.

Seeds are so small and once they are planted, grow invisibly for so long. For so long they are still and silent, for so long they seem dead. Until one day, when the sun and air and soil reach their tenuous agreements, the seed breaks down, breaks open, breaks into life. The edges that have held and protected fall away. The secrets held within the stillness and the silence spill out, destroying old worlds and creating new ones. All bargains of disappearance, safety, and smallness are broken and betrayed as boundaries are crossed from within the small seed into the soil, into the air, into the world. In a mighty act of creative transgression, life within the seed unfurls itself.

# LIFE TRANSGRESSES

*Living organisms have an inherent potential for
reaching out beyond themselves to create new
structures and new patterns of behavior.*

**Fritjof Capra**[6]

Life transgresses everywhere.

Life crosses over the assigned boundaries, disrupting old forms and destroying the edges of the familiar as it pushes past symmetry and stability into imbalance and chaos. And in the reaching, in the crossing over, life continues to unfold through the cycles of death and rebirth.

The word *transgress* comes from the Latin word *transgressus* or *transgredi* and means to step (*trans*) across (*gredi*), to go beyond or to cross imposed limits. It is interesting that this act of stepping away from the well-worn path has become so strongly associated with morality and is often defined as wrongdoing, sin, offense, and violation. We have taken transgression—the stepping beyond and across—and equated it with evil. This understanding of transgression as evil is not coincidental, since hierarchical systems of power-over rely heavily upon blind obedience, judgment, and fear. They need us to stay within the lines, to comply. They need us to stay obedient.

We have often equated disobedience with evil. But they are not the same thing.

In my life, transgression first came, not as behaviors or actions, but as forbidden questions and a need to tell the truth of what I felt and saw, even if it did not comply with the story I was supposed to tell.

During the years leading up to that fateful Tuesday night and to my Great Unraveling, I went on a night walk. Walking on the wide concrete sidewalks of southern California, I was trying to feel the night, the wind, the comfort of the dark. The unrest in me had been getting louder, writhing in my chest—it was serpentine. Things that had made sense didn't make sense anymore. I longed to fall into the fierceness of this unnamable longing, but I did not know how. As I walked, a knowing took over me.

I understood suddenly that I had been given so many answers without the questions. I realized that I had been living answers to questions I had never really asked. Not only had I never been taught to ask them, I had been discouraged from asking them, even as I memorized and recited the answers of my childhood. I knew in that moment I could no longer continue living this way. Something in me was breaking open and the questions would become my guides.

As I walked, I made a vow, a prayer: I would never again claim an answer to a question I had not asked, to a question I had not lived. I wanted to fall into them. Truthfully, I had no choice. Hovering above the questions and constantly propitiating against them was making me exhausted. My life could no longer be a walking announcement of The Answers. My life would become an act of devotion to the questions. Later, Rilke's words—*live the questions, live everything*—would rage across my thirsty heart, carving out a compass where there was no map.

It still astounds me that some believe the mysteries are afraid of our questions. I think maybe our honest true questions are one of their deepest delights—a form of true worship, a beautiful communion. And if the mysteries are not afraid, why should we be afraid? Is life that fragile? Are truths that brittle?

If what we have based our lives upon cannot withstand a childlike curiosity and a fierce commitment to the questions growing from the depths of our being, maybe we should let ourselves fall through those lives. Perhaps those are the moments when we allow the questions to do the sacred work of destruction. Perhaps this is when we reach for what is calling. Perhaps this is when we reach for what we long for, even if this longing might become a song of grief among the ruins of what we had known.

This is when we will no longer be named the holy sacrifice.

This is when we name ourselves.

The new sciences are showing us this archetypal pattern of creative transgression as foundational to the evolution of Nature. For centuries, the dominant Western narratives have been telling stories about how things are solid and separate. They have been telling us stories about how only what is permanent is real and only what is stable is trustworthy. They have populated the landscapes of our vision with images made of stone, unchanging and firm. Truth as immovable and permanent noun. We have been indoctrinated to see a world that obeys and to believe that we, too, must obey. Our Mother tells us a different story.

Nature is telling us a story of a reality that is a deeply interconnected, relational, dynamic and fluid. Nature is telling a story of a realm that is continually unfolding, continually spiraling through the cycles of death and rebirth, continually transforming by reaching beyond the boundaries of the status quo. The new sciences confirm over and over that living systems must break out of imposed or pre-established forms in order to reach higher complexity.[7]

This process is so important to the creative evolution of all things that in the past several decades some physicists have come to recognize this break of symmetry, this transgressive force, as the "key to the existence of our cosmos."[8] As living systems break through old structures, new life emerges. The breaking through and the crossing over—the transgression—can be found at the heart of our evolution. Without the ability of living systems to break away and to cross over assigned boundaries, the continual turning of life would cease. Nature is showing us a vision of reality as an ever-moving and dynamic verb.

At the heart of the predominant creation myth of the Western tradition lives a great creative transgression that still reverberates throughout our cultures, religions, and families: Eve reaching for the forbidden fruit. In fact, this kind of transgression is portrayed over and over in myths: Psyche taking the oil lamp into that dark room to look upon her lover's face, Ariadne consulting with Daedalus to help Theseus defeat the Minotaur and take her off her Father's island, and Eve reaching for the forbidden fruit because she saw that it was beautiful, nourishing, and carrier of knowing. Creative transgression is a movement that both destroys old forms and creates new possibilities.

These mysteries of our psychological, spiritual, and physical processes are etched within our bodies, reflected in our myths, and unfolding in the depths of the Earth. And what we witness is this: new knowing and new ways of being emerge out of transgression, that is, out of a stepping beyond prescribed or stable forms and a crossing over pre-assigned boundaries. The transgression at the center of our creation story has much to teach us about this essential rhythm of Nature.

# CREATION STORIES & ORIGINS

*Like Creation stories everywhere, cosmologies are a source
of identity and orientation to the world. They tell us
who we are. We are inevitably shaped by them no matter
how distant they may be from our consciousness.*

**Robin Wall Kimmerer**[9]

I was taught the Eden story from a young age. I knew that Eve had
listened to the devil disguised as a serpent, taken the forbidden fruit,
convinced Adam to take the fruit, and then been cursed and banished from paradise forever. I knew that because of Eve we all were
born depraved and in need of salvation. I understood that because of
Eve, woman was inferior and fated to be subjugated.

Even though everyone in the Western tradition isn't taught this
myth overtly, it is still significant to all of us because our creation
myths have to do with how we imagine our place in the world and
how we set up our societies. Even if you haven't overtly known this
myth like I have, I want to tell you about it and tend it with you
because it has shaped the way we have imagined and structured so
much of our lives—from churches and governments to family structure. It has been used as proof that we cannot trust our bodies, our
desires, and our instincts (especially if you are born female). It has
been used as the justification not only for the violence of sexism, but
also for horrors of racism and slavery. It has been used as a powerful
weapon to turn us against Nature—human and more-than-human
nature.[10]

The traditional interpretation of this story has infused our vision of ourselves and our body/Earth home with fallenness, depravity, and scarcity. Religious views of our nature as inherently evil, capitalistic commandments that we must always have more, patriarchal policies that enforce power-over, and wellness ideologies that have us constantly striving for improvement are all permeated and fueled by the belief that we are not okay as we are and that we will only be okay if we are somehow saved from our own nature and from Nature. And our creation story is one part of this—an important part.

The psychologist and scholar Marie-Louise von Franz wrote that creation myths are the "deepest and most important of all myths" and "refer to the most basic problems of human life, for they are concerned with the ultimate meaning, not only of *our* existence, but of the existence of the whole cosmos."[11] They have an instrumental and dialogical relationship with our ways of being in the world, interacting with and informing our conceptions about our daily struggles and our imagination around the nature of reality. In other words, we cannot escape our origins.

Not only are creation myths central to our "identity and orientation to the world,"[12] as Robin Wall Kimmerer put it, but also from a depth psychological sensibility, we understand all myths as expressions of the depths telling us about themselves—the wild self speaking of itself in disguise, showing us something of the mysteries of psyche and Nature. Myths show us timeless, universal patterns clothed in time, place, and culture specific garments. Carl Jung called these timeless dominant principles archetypes. He distinguished the archetype itself from archetypal images. Archetypes themselves, he wrote, are universal, timeless, and ultimately unknowable. Therefore, we can only approximate these mysteries partially through archetypal images, which are the time, place, and culture specific ways these ineffable "living dispositions" of the psyche make themselves known to us.[13] We can imagine myths as archetypal images that draw us closer to sacred patterns of psyche and Nature. They are not literal truths—they are metaphoric truths. They are particular and specific scenes that point us toward a universal and timeless experience.

As we befriend myths and cultivate a mythic sensibility, we are more able to see through the surface of things into the numinous and learn to "appreciate the divine in everyday."[14] A mythic sensibility opens up hidden doors and lures us into dusty magical wardrobes that take us into other dimensions of our lives. It brings us closer to our belonging in the depth and metaphoric realms of our experiences. A mythic sensibility allows us to see beyond the overt into the heart of things.

In a culture that over-emphasizes the overt—fiercely defending the view that what is most real and true is only that which can be measured, tested, and repeated—we have been marooned on the surface of things while the depths stir with the oceanic and untamed wildness of psyche and Nature. Left without images—the language of the soul—we are left with a poverty of expressive possibilities. By *image* I do not mean only a perceptual visual image, but rather a "small piece of imagination."[15] Images reach beyond and beneath language and explanation, offering us small vessels filled with experience drenched in imagination. Without these portals that enable us to look beyond the surface of things, we may become severed from the depth and mythic dimensions of our lives and of reality.

The first violence done to and with the Eden story is that it has been literalized. In other words, rather than being looked at and understood with metaphoric sensibilities, we have made the myth a literal historical enactment and, therefore, forced Eve into the human realm as a universal representation of every woman, the original literal (fallen and guilty) female. This view has not only been used as reason and proof of our inherent depravity, it has also served as blank-slate rationale and justification for horrific ideologies of oppression and subjugation. In order for us to see through this rigid, burdensome, and harmful narrative, in order to tend to its illness and find its medicine, we must return Eve to the mythic realm where she belongs. Rather than reading myth as literal fact, we are invited to read myths as metaphoric mirrors of our experiences.

For example, Lilith, who is often offered as a counterpart to Eve, is a female mythic figure who kills babies, seduces men, has regular sexual intercourse with Satan, and births legions of demons.[16] She is, at first glance, a more terrifying and dangerous force than Eve. However, Lilith, unlike Eve, has remained primarily in her mythical home. That is, she is understood as a symbol and as a metaphor for aspects of our archetypal experiences. Since she has not been forced to bear the burdens of a literal interpretation and of being a universal stand in for all women, her life remains mostly in the imaginal realm, often taking us deeper into the experience of the hidden, true, and even terrifying aspects of our realities. On the other hand, because Eve has been literalized and made to represent all females, the deeper truths of the myth have been exiled into the unconscious, leaving us with superficial, literal interpretations that serve as barriers to the deeper archetypal invitations of the myth.

In the Western tradition, Adam and Eve—Clay Man and Bone Woman—are our mythic origins and it is not enough to simply embrace them or turn away from them, because since they have been literalized into concrete and historical fact, *we do not know them.* When we deny our myths, we deny our metaphoric roots. A return to our myths and to a mythic perspective empowers us to look beyond the surface of life and into the stories that are living through us. As our vision enlarges, we are offered the opportunity to understand the greater contexts within which we are embedded and to participate in our deepest belonging.

I am not, as feminist Mary Daly warned against, trying to "depatriarchalize" the myth in a gross denial of the sexism inherent in it.[17] We live with that sexism; we suffer its consequences and we do not forget nor look away. We cannot deny the profoundly harmful ways this myth has been used to shape our systems of hierarchy and power-over. Nor should we. But we can look again. We can look more closely at what is buried in the myth. We can return it to its mythic and imaginal home.

When a myth is torn from its metaphoric home—*where it is always fluid, multiple, and dynamic in its meanings*—and literalized into historical fact and singular prescriptive interpretation, it begins to act, at best, as a splint or rigid boundary constricting and limiting our natural movements, cycles, and transformations. At its worst, it becomes a powerful weapon of oppression. As the images harden under the pressure of literalization, their translucence fades and becomes opaque. They become petrified and inert on the outside. We can no longer see through them.

Images made of stone cease to tell their truths; they are trapped, and they entrap. I wonder if this is the truest meaning of idolatry: to cast our images into stone and entrap them in a too small and singular perspective. Eve has been stolen from the great halls of mythic memory and has been cast into stone and forced to stand in as Everywoman. Her stone figure has served as reminder of the depravation of all of creation, and we have lived in its shadow. But images cast in stone are not dead, they are only waiting. Waiting for the return of our mythic sight. Waiting to be re-baptized in the Holy Imagination.

Eve is not the only significant mythic figure that has suffered in the confinement of literalization. Mary the Mother has also been memorialized in stone, not only keeping us from the metaphoric medicine of this mythic figure but also keeping females firmly in an impossible binary: Eve or Mary.

# MOTHER MARY

*We need images and myths through which we can
see who we are and what we might become.*

**Christine Downing**[18]

On a soft day, the kind of day that comes when summer is turning
into autumn in the Pacific Northwest, I danced my prayers in my
small living room—I danced grief, frustration, desire, joy. And in
the dance that afternoon, Mary found me. Even though I had heard
of her since infancy, on this day I met her. Just as some feel the need
to turn away from Eve because she carries our wounded stories, so
I had felt the need to turn away from Mary. Even though so many
have found comfort and strength in the mythic image of the mother
of Christ and image of feminine sacredness, I felt mostly her silence
and her complacency as she stood by quietly and obediently as her
son was murdered on a cross, as the story tells us. I couldn't connect
with her bodiless holiness and sexless purity. But when I met Mary
that afternoon—the archetypal Mary that visits as psycho-spiritual
force and presence—I realized again the theft of a literalized and
impoverished imagination. I felt the grief over what is stolen from
us when our images of the sacred are literalized, and therefore, rendering their vast metaphoric wisdom into constrictive idioms and
dogmas.

As a little girl I knew what the dream for my life should be: finding the perfect God-like husband and filling a modest house with
spirited but obedient children, preferably with a male firstborn. No

one told me this directly, but it was in the air. But this is not what I dreamt about. I dreamt of adventure, of daring, of exploration, of having power and sovereignty over my own life. I still kept the dreams within the bounds of what was approved by imagining that all my adventures would be for God and in an effort to save the world, and that since I could not be sovereign over my own life, I planned on choosing a man who wanted exactly what I wanted and so would lead me into the life I chose. I would follow his lead into my own dreams. I had found a hack, a loophole.

Although this mostly worked to appease my unrest, sometimes the fallacy of this plan would show through in the thought that, ultimately, I wish I had been born a man. Not because I wanted to be a different gender or in a different body, but because I wanted to have sovereignty. I wanted to have voice. I wanted to have opportunity. And this was for men. I did not have a strong desire to be wife and mother, to be powerful only in the approved realms of womanhood. And into my twenties, even after I married very young, I still felt ambivalent about having children. Slowly I grappled with my fears and untangled the narratives that kept me from knowing what I desired until one day when I was twenty-nine, I knew. I knew in my bones.

My husband and I lived in a purple house on the top of one of the seven Seattle hills in a tiny attic apartment. When we moved in, I immediately painted the living room walls dark red. I knew on some level I was in a season of birthing myself into the world. On this day when I was twenty-nine, I was awake in bed in this tiny red apartment when suddenly I heard it. I heard the call from my child, not as a literal voice but as a deep intuitive sense: *It's time.* And I knew this was true. I wanted this little one. It would be six years before I met my son in this world. I waited through these years and the call stayed with me, and from that day on I missed him every day.

First, my husband wanted us to buy a house. Soon, we moved into a small, old charcoal grey house. I loved this small house, creaky and full of quirks. Again, I immediately painted the living room walls a deep red, another womb. And indeed, when I moved out of this house after over a decade, I realized that this house had held me like a womb—it had kept me safe while it made me.

Almost a year after moving into our house, I became pregnant. Finally, I would meet this little one. I took the test, "pregnant." My husband went to the store and got more tests and we took others. All positive. We hugged, jumped up and down, we cried, we made love. I wondered if my body would be able to sustain this life, to hold it and nurture it. It wasn't.

Within a week I had severe cramping and went into the ER. This began several weeks of uncertainty and waiting. Weeks of pain and debilitating nausea. Until finally the miscarriage. I was up all night in terrible pain as my body was emptied, emptiness upon emptiness. Weeks and weeks of bleeding as my reluctant uterus tried to hold on, to not let go. I felt utterly powerless and utterly empty. After being emptied out, I crashed into the bottom of my sense of powerlessness and, I knew what my task would be: I must name myself.

During one of the bleeding days of the bleeding weeks, I lay in bed swimming in hopelessness and sadness, when out of the center of my body an image, a thought, a visitor arose—the Ash tree. I don't know how, but suddenly the Ash Tree was with me. From my bed, I began feverishly researching this tree. The Ash Tree signifies rebirth and the healing of the womb. It grows near flowing waters. Lives mostly in the underworld. Explosive. Poetic. The connection between the seen and the unseen, matter and spirit. It is known as the Tree of Life, the axis mundi that connects worlds. For those who are uprooted. For those who need to be connected. Ash Tree met me in my despair and gave me hope, lifted me up. She taught me what I needed to be in that moment.

I spent a long Seattle winter inside, quietly healing. I began to truly name myself, telling the truth of my experiences in the quiet of my own heart and on the pages of my journal. I found out that going home was possible for me. On the due date of that pregnancy we planted an Ash tree behind our house and now it towers over the house and shades the small sunroom where I've spent countless hours dreaming, weeping, studying, and waiting.

Almost a year after the miscarriage, we decided we were ready to try again. I missed my son now more than ever. Moon after moon, the blood came. All around me wombs were fertile, and babies were brought into the world. Mothers were being made before my eyes. But my womb remained empty. My longing for my son became a tangible truth I carried around with me like searing fire in my palms. Sometimes it felt unbearable, the longing. Two years went by, month by month, blood by blood, moon by moon. I began to allow other dreams to populate my future. But I never stopped longing.

With each moon cycle, my sense of control melted away exposing my vulnerability and stripping away layers of efforting as I realized how hard you have to try when you think you are in control. One day, as I sat on my big brown couch, the reality of pregnancy itself taught me profound lessons.

When a woman is pregnant, she doesn't wake up one day and think, *Today I will make a toe or an arm*. She nurtures; she holds. She waits while something is made in the dark. She supports the process, she endures the process, she allows the process, but she does not orchestrate the creation nor effort her way into a new life. The impulse towards life takes over until finally in an ultimate act of surrender, the woman gives her body over to the shudders of life and death, she opens as new life passes through.

How often, however, the illusion of making, controlling, efforting permeates our fantasies not only of physical pregnancy, but also of psycho-spiritual pregnancy, of invisible transformation and birth. I was deeply aware of this fantasy in my own life, i.e., that it was all up to me if only I tried hard enough and worked hard enough. Yet, the body was teaching me something different about the mysteries of our unfolding. Profound participation, communion, and surrender:

yes. Conjuring through effort and control: no. I was suddenly filled with an urgent craving for my body to be covered in mud, as I was filled with this sense of surrender to the deep wisdom of Nature.

I went to the local co-op and bought a jar of clay. I filled our spare room with all the plants in the house, I lit candles and incense, I played soft music, I turned on my small space heater, and placed a blanket at the center of the room and turned off the lights. Then, I ceremoniously spread clay all over my naked body and lay there on that blanket. Over an hour or two, I felt the clay harden as it pulled at my skin. I laid there alone in that dim room being made and unmade, exposed and covered, surrendering to the mysteries of transformation. After the clay was completely dry and when I was ready, I stepped into the shower and watched as the waters slowly washed away the grey-brown clay, a baptism in mud and water. I repeated this ritual throughout the week and at the end of that week found out I was pregnant.

On another Tuesday, as the autumn had begun to descend, I noticed some cramping. It felt familiar. With shaking hands, I took the test. Pregnant. And this time, I would finally meet him.

The next June, my beautiful son was born on a Tuesday morning. His father and I tenderly held him and gazed at him, remembering how long we had waited. Years later, we would sit in our tiny backyard and watch our son, Asher, play on a swing hung from a branch of the Ash tree we had planted, feeling the depth of meaning of this moment, taking nothing for granted.

To be mother, to be mothered, to be named, to have voice, to have sovereignty even as I surrendered to the mysteries crashing into my life as fate—my journey toward Mother was drenched in longing, in naming and un-naming, filling and emptying. So, on the rainy day when I first met Mary the Mother, my heart was full and ready to feel her kind of mothering, to be at once mothered and mother in her powerful self-belonging.

In Mary I felt the great beating heart of the fierce and grieving Mother who wants only nurture and love for her children; I felt the warmth of the expansive heart that is able to hold so much. As my body moved in maternal gestures, I felt both mothered and mother. In Mary I felt the power that creates life in and through herself—the one-in-herselfness Esther Harding describes as the true meaning of virginity.[19] I met Mary the Virgin Mother, the mother that *belongs to herself* and from her place of sovereignty gives of herself to her children. I felt her love and power course through my body as I danced, as I worshipped, as I loved her even as her love broke down the walls of my resistance.

As I considered this experience with Mary, I was struck again by her own burden of literalization. The literalized Mary is the submissive female who gives birth without being defiled by sex and desire; she offers females a way toward salvation, that is, sexless procreation and passive compliance. The literalized Mary—who holds her grief silently in her heart as she witnesses horrors of injustice, the murder of her own son—is the image of the purified female who ascends into heaven without body and without death. If Eve is the fallen female in the fullness of depraved sexual power and animal instinct, Mary is the elevated female in the glory of spirit free of body.

In this unimaginative and literalized understanding, body, sex, blood, and desire were placed upon Eve when she reached for and ate the forbidden fruit. Spirit, purity, and salvation were offered to Mary when she birthed a sinless child, who would also be imagined as sex-less. Eve rebelled; Mary watched in silent obedience. Eve was cursed with pain in childbirth; Mary remained chaste and, so, offered salvation to humanity.

Just as Jesus has been imagined as the second Adam, redeeming men from the burdens of sin, so Mary has been imagined as the second Eve. Mary ascends in sexless, bodiless purity, leaving Eve and all females on the earth in the inglorious cycles of death and rebirth, in the realities of blood and sex. Not only is this binary problematic in that we are all bodies that bleed, desire, and live in the mess and mud of the earth, thus, rendering the only acceptable image of being female completely unattainable, it is also problematic in that it offers only two images, two ways.

Let us shatter these literalized images and watch the pieces become as multiple as the stars shining in the dark skies, singing their songs of multiplicity. We join their chorus, giving voice to the countless ways of being female and the countless currents of feminine processes running through us, regardless of biological sex. Let the shattering not only be a return to the deep archetypal and ancient wisdom of our mythic mothers, Eve and Mary, freeing them from concrete prisons of idolatry—images cast in stone—let it also break our imagination free from the prisons of restrictive binaries and literalized mythic images.

The legacy of this split binary image for females—Virgin or Whore—has been violent and brutal. Christine Downing reminds us, "We need images and myths through which we can see who we are and what we might become."[20] We must move toward many voices, myths, stories, archetypal images, and ways of being, emphasizing a continual need to not make one image the normative one but to engage in true plurality.

There have been attempts along the way to integrate images of the feminine sacred, and therefore the sacrilized female body, into our religious imagination. In Christianity we have Mary, the submissive, silent, eternal virgin. In mystical Judaism we find *Shekhina*, the feminine immanence of God among his people. In Islam we find Fatima, the divine woman who is freed from the burdens of menstruation and menopause and gives birth from her thigh with intact virginity. Archetypally, we may understand these appearances as the psyche making known what has been neglected or forgotten, in this case a sacred sense of woman and all that has been associated with the idea of the feminine.

However, these attempts toward the reintegration and redemption of Eve and of feminine sacred ways remained within spiritual and psychological realms, with images of the acceptable feminine still purged of sexuality, blood, and body. Eve herself remained with all female bodies in the glorious realities of blood, childbirth, sex, and desire. Eve began the conversation but was left behind in the purification of the feminine in male-centric paradigms.

But, remember, the Eden story is homeopathic: it carries our illness and our medicine. As we move from a literal approach to a mythic sensibility, perhaps we can see into the shadows of the story, beyond the overt and into its metaphoric depths.

I want to tell you a story about what is buried in the Eden myth. It is a story intended as a burial of death—as an eternal exile of the wisdom within it—but it became a burial of protection instead.

This story became a seed planted in the dark.

# THE FORGOTTEN GODDESS

*At the very dawn of religion, God was a woman. Do you remember?*

**Merlin Stone**[21]

Long ago, creation myths all over the world spoke of a great Mother Goddess birthing creation into being. Born of her womb, creation was made of the substance—the blood, flesh, and bones—of the goddesses. Creation was an act of embodiment and incarnation. We were offspring of the goddesses and the gods. Then, slowly but steadily, across many world mythologies creation stories began to shift. Mythologist Joseph Campbell called this shift the Great Reversal.

Images of the great Creatrix Goddess birthing creation from her own womb were replaced by images of the Sky Father speaking creation into being through his word. No longer the offspring of the Great Mother, Creation became product. No longer made of the same substance as the sacred, no longer flesh of her flesh and blood of her blood, Creation became the technology of the gods: separate, spiritless, and ultimately fallen.

For example, in Sumeria the god Enlil slowly absorbed the three creator goddesses—Ninhursag, An, and Enki—and spoke all things into being. In the Mesopotamian creation story "Enuma Elish" we find Marduk battling Tiamat and eventually tearing her body into two pieces, heaven and earth. In Egypt, two thousand years before Genesis, the god Ptah also created the world through his word, again appropriating the creative powers of the goddesses. And in the predominant creation story in the Western tradition, Yahweh speaks the world into being, usurping the powers of fertility and creation from the Goddess.

All across the region, the goddesses were being defeated, pushed underground. Of course, in some cultures their stories were never forgotten, and to those cultures and memory keepers we owe deep gratitude.[22] But for those in the Western Christian tradition, these stories disappeared into the mists of time. The fading was neither gentle nor natural. Fierce battles were waged—are waged—to keep these stories buried. The Eden story is a part of this larger mythological movement. However, the Eden story is unique in that it could not afford to admit the presence of other deities, not even the Goddess, since the movement in this case not only involved establishing Yahweh as Creator but also as the only God. In the story of the Garden of Eden the move was being made not only from Creatrix to Creator but also from the many to the one.

In the Eden myth, no Goddess—no images of the feminine sacred—is allowed to exist. She cannot be named nor fought, since to name her, even if only to defeat her, would be to admit her presence and importance. How could Yahweh fight and defeat the Goddess if her existence could not be acknowledged? The Goddess in the Eden story had to be dispossessed of her powers without being made visible. She had to be defeated without being named.

This is the battle that wages at the heart of the Eden story. Buried within the myth is the Goddess in the Garden: Asherah.

Asherah is mentioned forty times in the Old Testament. The worship and veneration of the Goddess was an integral part of the Hebrew culture at the time when the Eden story came into consciousness, around 900 BCE.[23] She was worshipped in high places, where one would find representations of the Goddess referred to as *asherahs*—sometimes a statue shaped like a tree, at other times an actual tree.

Biblical texts themselves prove the importance of Asherah to the Hebrew people, with the prophets' continual demands for the destruction of the asherahs and veiled warnings against her veneration.[24]

Yahweh, a god who most likely originated from the Median region, was easily introduced into the polytheistic pantheon of the Canaanites, which was ruled by the god El. From this position, Yahweh slowly merged with El and eventually absorbed El almost completely. In fact, biblical patriarchal narratives show that the first name the Hebrews ascribed to their god was El, reflected in the name Israel itself, meaning "God [El] strives (or rules)."[25] This is significant because it was well known that Asherah was partner to El, a fact that sheds light on how she remained on as an indispensable consort to Yahweh for so long.

Yahweh and Asherah were often worshipped together and were most likely seen as complementary rather than competitive forces. Often asherahs would be found next to stone pillars, which stood as representations of Yahweh. Archeological discoveries have found evidence of asherahs in Yahweh's temples in Samaria and Jerusalem. It is very likely that Asherah was widely known to the Hebrew people as Yahweh's consort, that is, Yahweh's wife. In fact, there is no evidence that prior to the Eden story there were any formal prohibitions against her worship.

The Eden story marks a point when the prophets and priests of Yahweh began a long and hard-fought war against the Goddess Asherah. Hebrew scholar Rafael Patai concluded that although the worship of Asherah spanned six centuries (continuing long after the Eden story), intermittently but with "gradually increasing intensity and frequency" the prophets and priests demanded the worship of Yahweh as the one and only deity.[26] As the prophetic demand for monotheistic Yahweh worship increased, the campaign against the Goddess eventually succeeded in eradicating much of the evidence of her religion, appropriating her symbols and practices, and associating her with an "abomination."[27]

Since Yahweh had to defeat Asherah without admitting her existence, the first step toward dethroning Asherah was to cast her into human form: Eve. In order for the Eden story to serve as a warning against her worship, Asherah had to be recognizably present even without being named. Asherah was forced to roam the shadows of the Garden, her story written in invisible ink with the symbols in the myth: serpent, tree, fruit, and even in her name. A closer look at these symbols not only unearths her presence in the Garden, but also reveals her (and Eve's) belonging in a long line of Earth Mother goddesses.

In the traditional and literalized interpretation of the story, symbols like the tree and the serpent have been orphaned from their mythological context and made to mirror the patriarchal views projected onto them. And yet, re-membering the Eden story back to its archetypal and mythic background allows us to see the symbols more clearly. For example, the serpent has been made to represent the devil and depraved sexuality, but seen in the whole context of its mythic belonging, the serpent can be recognized as one of the oldest personifications of the feminine sacred and as an enduring symbol of the mysteries of death, rebirth, and self-regeneration.

Although the story attempts to erase Asherah without naming her, the names themselves begin to weave a binding spell between Eve and Asherah. Eve's name, "Life" or "She who gives life,"[28] weaves her to Asherah who was also known as "Lifegiver."[29] After the curses are pronounced, Adam named Eve "The Mother of All the Living," which further strengthens Eve's bonds with Asherah because this title was an ancient and well-known "honorific epithet" of the Goddess.[30] It points us toward the Goddess in the shadows of the Garden and reveals Eve's belonging in a long and ancient line of Near Eastern mother goddesses.[31] Not all goddesses were mother goddesses, but significantly, Asherah was. She was known as "Progenitress of the Gods" and as "Mother of the Gods."[32] In her lowliest and most humiliated moment, Eve was given a title that evoked the Goddess and thereby both were called fallen, submissive, and weak.

Although Asherah is not directly named in the myth, as we return this story to its mythic and archetypal context, we continue to find her solidly at the center of the story: the sacred tree. The sacred tree was an ancient symbol associated with the Goddess. Trees were commonly planted in Goddess temples, and some goddesses, like Hathor, Nut, and Isis, were known as "Lady of the Sycamore."[33] At that time, Asherah was symbolically interchangeable with the sacred tree. Often her places of worship were trees in high places. This is where her followers went to worship her. Across the region, the sacred tree symbolized her divinity, knowledge, wisdom, oracular knowing, enlightenment, and revelation. In another shrouded but firm move, the sacred tree of the Goddess became the bringer of death.

Asherah's exile continues with the vilification of the serpent. For millennia, the serpent has represented the Goddess. Many goddesses, including Asherah, were called "Serpent Lady."[34] Sometimes the goddesses themselves, like Tiamat, have taken the form of the serpent or dragon. The serpent has long been the ancient guardian of the Tree of Life. Before the Eden story, the image of the serpent guarding the sacred tree was at least a thousand years old. It is significant to notice that the imagery that connects the Goddess to the serpent and to the tree are nearly identical: cyclical death and rebirth, the life principle, self-regeneration, and divination.

Here we arrive at the center of the transgression: taking in the forbidden fruit. This fruit, most likely a fig, is at the heart of this story. Asherah is not only deeply entangled and present in this myth through the sacred tree and the serpent, she is also invoked through the fruit. The fruit was a place of sacred communion in her worship rituals. Asherah was known as the Branch Goddess and her worshipers would sit together and pass a branch laden with fruit around the circle. Each participant would take a bite from the fruit, partaking in the "flesh and the fluid of the Goddess."[35] Fruits and nuts from sacred trees were taken in as offerings from her body and this intimate act of communion, eating fruit from the sacred tree, would impart some of her numinosity and power. To take in the fruit of the Branch Goddess was to take in her flesh and her fluid, to transfer some of her power into your own body.

Of course, this is reminiscent of the later Christian communion ritual where the body of Christ is taken in through bread and wine and reflects significant shifts in the move from Earth Goddess to Sky God consciousness. Whereas in Goddess rituals, worshipers sat in circles and ate the fruit directly from the branch, in God rituals worshipers tend to sit in rows facing the higher authority (who is usually elevated, closer to the Sky Father) and take in more processed forms of the fruit and grain. In both cases, partaking of the fruit is imagined as union with the divine.

When Eve reached for that fruit, she was taking in the flesh and fluid of the Goddess, partaking of her body. This is transgression as communion. Eve's transgression was a moment of severance from the old way of the Garden and a moment of participation in the mysteries of the Goddess as she took in her flesh and fluid. And once she took in this power, Eve was transformed. She saw the world in a new way, her eyes were opened. The serpent's words emerged as true: Eve and Adam had become like the gods.

After the transgression, the gods convened. Suddenly Yahweh was not alone and gathered with other gods. The conversation the gods had at the end of this myth is a powerful portal into the mythological significance of this transgressive story. The gods expressed concern and alarm because now that they had taken in the flesh of the fruit, Eve and Adam had become like them. And the gods were afraid that they would eat from the Tree of Life and live forever, like them.

Were the gods protecting their power? Were the gods in some

way protecting Eve and Adam's humanity? We don't know. But the myth does make very clear that they were cast out because now they knew too much. Although we have been told over and over that they were exiled because they had become impure, sexual, and depraved death-bringers, the myth clearly tells us otherwise. What we see in the myth is that they were exiled not because they had become impure but because they had become like the gods: knowing and sovereign.

In this myth, not only were the serpent, the tree, and the fruit not named sacred, they became the carriers of death and exile. To listen to the serpent would be a grave error. To participate in the life of this tree would be to transgress. To take the fruit would be to invite certain death. The serpent and the tree—ancient symbols associated with the goddesses as representations of self-renewing life force, wisdom, fertility, and knowing—became the bringers of death, exile, and shame. But seeds hold and keep buried life safe enough until the time is right, until it is time to remember.

# RE-MEMBERING

*To remember is to be remembered, to have our own lives
made whole and our connections with others healed.*

## Christine Downing[36]

In my early thirties one of my deep longings was named: I wanted
the feminine sacred and I wanted to re-member myself to my deepest belonging. I longed for images that would reflect back to me my
own sacredness and the sacredness of Nature—body and Earth. I
was thirsty for other ways of knowing and being. I had been wandering in the underworld for years and my eyes had grown accustomed
to the dark, and in the shadows, I glimpsed her form. In the shadows
with the Goddess, I sensed her—I sensed my wild self—and my
hunger became ravenous.

A dear friend and I decided we would put together a year of studying the feminine sacred together. We scoured the bibliographies of
our favorite related books and followed the trails. We put together a
reading schedule for the year and embarked on our self-made journey
toward the Goddess. It was a magical year as we traversed the edges of
what we had known and discovered that beyond those edges there was
more. It was a tragic year as we traced the edges of the injustices that
kept us small and used. It was a triumphant year as we transgressed beyond those stories, names, and curses and discovered a fertile and wild
Vastness beyond those edges. We felt both our joy and our sorrow, as
we followed our longing and re-membered her and ourselves.

We went far into the myths of the goddesses, into theologies that included the feminine and females, and into practices of the feminine sacred. We traveled through stories about moon rituals and dark damp caves. We physically walked multiple labyrinths, letting our bodies teach us a new way of moving and knowing. After months of reading, reflection, and hours and hours of conversation, we gathered ourselves on an island in the Puget Sound and under a circle of trees we held ceremony.

All our travels to her led us to the center of our own beings. Our travels to her led us to our bodies, our longing, our hunger, our knowing, our belonging. We no longer had to be on the spiritual periphery. The images and myths and ways of the feminine sacred invited us into our wild belonging in the life of all things. We were invited into a way of being that is interconnected, fluid, dynamic, and multiple. We were taught about the wisdom of the dark and the value of descent. Remembering her helped us re-member ourselves to the wildness we belong to.

I grew up immersed in biblical teachings. I read the Bible regularly and carefully myself. I even went to a college that required all of its students to minor in biblical studies. And yet, Asherah was not mentioned to me, not even once. I did not notice her, not even once. But I missed her. I waited for her—an image of sacredness that included me and that showed me my own sacredness. I lived with a hunger for an image of the sacred that would invite me into the conversation, not as other but as kin. And she was right there all along.

Buried within the myth is the Goddess in the Garden: Asherah. Eve leads us to her, and we remember. Not in order to confine her to a literal prison and reduce her to a factual or historical truth for, again, *we speak not of goddesses but of mysteries.* To confuse and conflate the images—the ways we know—with the mysteries—the things we are knowing—is to succumb to deadening fundamentalisms.

We remember because the images of the great creatrix goddesses, images of these sacred archetypal patterns and processes running through our lives and histories, are stories about our own sacredness and our own belonging. To remember her is to remember ourselves. To remember her is to remember parts of our own nature that have been exiled and buried with her. To find her buried in the shadows is to work toward our own resurrection; it is to unearth ways of being and knowing that were exiled and buried long ago. It is to engage in the ritual of remembering ourselves and each other.

These are stories about ways of being and knowing that are radically different than the ways of being and knowing that are favored in the style of consciousness based on hierarchical power-over that we call the patriarchy. Although these ways of being and knowing were bound to the ankles of the female body and to images of the goddesses when they were cast into the shadows of patriarchal consciousness, they do not belong only to female bodies or ideas of the feminine. They belong to all of us who want to expand and remember a way of being that values interconnection, fluidity, circularity, intimacy with the cycles of death and rebirth, somatic and imaginal wisdom, and multiplicity. They are for all of us who want to transgress the shoulds of hierarchical systems of power-over—which often cause us to live in a continual practice of exiling parts of ourselves, our experiences, and each other into the shadows—and step into more expansive ways of living as we welcome more of ourselves home.

Looking at Eve's transgression in the Garden with an archetypal and mythic lens—rather than with a literal and historical approach—offers us a profound opportunity for this re-membering. Right here in the heart of a myth that has been used as a weapon against our wholeness, we find what has been lost in the shadows for so long. Buried within the story of Eve's transgression, we find ways of being that value immanence as well as transcendence. Looking with mythic vision, we see ways of being that have relinquished the exclusive worship of ascension and know how to surrender to the descent as we are initiated into deeper and more expansive ways of living. We are re-membered back to ways of being that invite us to continually move from devotion to The One Way into the honoring of the many ways—from linear singularity to spiraling multiplicity. Buried below the surface of the myth are ways of being that know how to see in the dark and how to grow down. These are ways of being that know how to dance with the rhythms of death and rebirth, know how to trust Body and commune with Nature. These are ways of being that invite us into our wild knowing.

# BOOK TWO:
## EVE'S WAYS OF BEING

*The transgression of Eve was an act of courage that led us out
of the garden into the wilderness... The moment Eve bit into
the apple, her eyes opened and she became free. She exposed
the truth of what every woman knows: to find our sovereign
voice often requires a betrayal. We just have to make certain
we do not betray ourselves... The snake who tempted Eve to eat
the forbidden fruit was not the Devil, but her own instinctive
nature saying,* Honor your hunger and feed yourself.

**Terry Tempest Williams**[37]

# THE GOOD GIRL

*Eden was over; life began.*

**James Hillman**[38]

She walked into the room and I was immediately mesmerized—tall and soft-spoken, probably in her seventies, she had *gravitas*. Strangely, I don't remember her name, but I remember what she brought me that afternoon. She was a guest speaker in one of my classes in my doctoral program, and she came to tell us her story.

In her mid-life her husband had become very ill. During the time of his illness and recovery, she had developed a particular way of painting—it was deeply spiritual and psychological—and had eventually written a book about this experience. On this afternoon, she brought the series of paintings from that time in her life to show us as she told us her story. They were beautiful. We sat in front of her in a semi-circle with the paintings in a semi-circle on the floor in front of us.

During her presentation, one of my classmates asked her something like, "What did you learn in this process?" or "How did this experience change you?" I leaned in, eager for her words. Her answer stunned me. She sat still, quiet, for a moment.

Then, with a smile on her face she slowly pointed at the first painting in the series, "Here I was a good girl…" then she traced the shape of the semi-circle as she followed the paintings on the floor until she reached the last one, "And here, I was no longer a good girl." My body awakened with recognition. I *knew* what she meant. I knew it in my cells and in my bones.

I went to university in Los Angeles. I experienced it as a vast landscape of suburban dreariness. Horizons filled with concrete, strip malls, and traffic. But one day, just north of the campus, I found a small oasis. There was a small tunnel, probably something to do with emergency drainage, at the edge of the parking lot of my dorm. It was circular and about twenty feet long and ten feet tall at the center. I discovered that if you walked through, it led to a beautiful narrow park nestled between rows of houses. There was a small creek running through it with picturesque bridges crossing over the waters. I couldn't believe it—this hidden green refuge right here! From then on, I would often walk halfway through the drainage passage and look back toward the campus, heat waves lifting off the concrete colorless surfaces. Then I would look toward the park, waters running through and vibrant green. It felt like magic every time. I felt like the children finding the wardrobe, pushing past the coats, and wandering accidentally into the otherworldliness of Narnia.

One day I wandered into that world with a good friend. We slowly walked through the passage and then sat on the small bridge, our legs dangling off the sides through the railing. For the first time I tried to put words to something growing in me: a profound exhaustion. I remember telling her it wasn't about doing all the things I needed to do, it was about not being able to be what I was supposed to be anymore. I didn't really even know what that meant exactly at the time. I just felt it so deeply. The seeds buried in my depths had begun to break open, pushing the boundaries of what I was supposed to be and breaking down the walls that had kept me safe but were now too small for what my life wanted to become.

When Eve found me, I was beginning to understand I would not be able to remain a good girl much longer. Not because I wanted to behave differently, but because I needed to be different. In my life, to be a good girl was to take up little space, ask only answerable, pre-approved questions, to mirror my elders, and above all, to stay within the lines, to obey. But my sense of life was spilling over. And I was running out of efforting willpower to continue to be that girl. I didn't rebel. I longed. And eventually I reached.

Often in myths, the lost quester must enter dark forests where there is no path. Here at the edge of this terrifying and dark forest, I caught glimpses of Eve in the shadows—she roams this edge between good and knowing.

I imagine her slow steps as she wanders through her paradise. Named. Safe. Obedient. Favored. She is a deeply embedded part of the hierarchy of the Garden: Yahweh, Adam, Eve, animals, and land. As I began to know the archetypal Eve, one of the first things I noticed is that her role was clearly defined: created out of the body of Adam by the Father God in order to be helper. She knows her place. It is clear and uncomplicated. Her name and her place are chosen by another. Until she listens to her body, her senses, her sight, and her desire.

If you have ever been good, you know there is a peace to knowing your place. There is a comfort in clarity. There is a certain calm in living an unquestioned life. But let us not be fooled. The cost of being named by another is high, even if that cost is sometimes invisible to the outside world or insignificant to anyone but our own wild self. Abandoning ourselves in our quest to find favor through compliance and obedience is very costly to our wild souls.

Thankfully, one day you may hear a small whisper calling you into transgression. You may listen to the instinctual animal body and you may look at what has been forbidden. You may see that it is beautiful. You may see that it offers knowing and nourishment. And you may reach and let the flesh of the fruit become a part of you. And as you feel the juices running down your neck, your eyes will be opened, and you will know. Yes, if this happens and you reach for what you desire, you will most likely lose much. You may also have the opportunity to name yourself and to live a life that is more free and more true.

I knew the artist that day was not talking about behaviors or lifestyles. I knew she was not talking about morality or evil.

"*Here I was a good girl.*" She was talking about living according to the expectations of others. She was talking about a life shaped by the external mandates of what she should be. She was speaking of the obedient life.

"*Here I was no longer a good girl.*" She was talking about self-belonging. She was talking about a life shaped by what wells up from her depths. She was talking about sovereignty. She was speaking of a life rooted in the soil of her own wild knowing.

# LIVING IN BETWEEN

*The path you took to get here has washed out;*
*The way forward is still concealed from you.*
*'The old is not old enough to have died away;*
*The new is still too young to be born.'*
**John O'Donohue**[39]

After that night when I whispered my vows to the questions, I continued to be unmade. On another night during this unraveling, I sat with a friend by the track of our small Christian university. In that dark quiet, I was trying to put words to the hole in my chest, to the deep loss I was falling into more each day, to the betrayal of being left by the God I had devoted my life too and who had defined everything about my world, abandoned to wander in unknowing. I was desperate for meaning. I was full of grief. I was consumed by this loss and it was sending me on a deep descent into the underworld, even as I prepared for my college graduation and upcoming wedding. My friend listened for a while and was mostly quiet, then very carefully and thoughtfully—I could tell she was nervous—said, "I don't see you longing for God. I don't see you seeking God. I don't see you trying."

During these years of unraveling, I felt so lost and the community around me had only one answer to the wrong question. They largely perceived my crisis as a lack of God. I knew in my bones I was sick with God; God was dissolving himself and myself into new forms and I was suffering God's dissolution with every breath. I wasn't turning away from that way of life. I was leaning into what was calling. I was surrendering to the relentless questions. It is not that I didn't miss the comfort and familiarity of my old way of being—the certainty and the favor—I did. Although there were many aspects of that way of being that harmed me and I could no longer tolerate, I had also loved it. I felt deeply conflicted. But my longing was stronger than obedience. It is not that I wasn't afraid—I was terrified. But the desire to live more freely in the truth of my experience was stronger than the fear. My devotion to the questions was stronger than my devotion to the answers. And, I was profoundly devasted.

Even while I was beckoned into a new way of living and viewing the world, I still longed for my place in the old one. I still wanted favor and belonging; I still wanted to be seen and validated in the old world. Especially at that time when I had no images of what could be possible. There was no map. There was no vision. There was no mirror. There was no hope of belonging. I was in a liminal place between worlds. And honestly, it often felt almost unbearable. For years.

Eve exists in these in–between spaces. Eve stands between the serpent and Adam and between Adam and Yahweh. She stands between what she has been told to live and feel and what she experiences through her body and her intuition. While she reaches for the fruit and shatters the form of her prior existence, she is still with Adam and still longs for Yahweh's approval. Eve was born from the womb of the Great Mother into the hands of the Sky Father. Birthed through Her and named by Him, her belonging is always ambiguous. Her loyalty is always in question. In belonging to both worlds,

she belongs to neither. Even now this ambiguous belonging and loyalty remains true.

While patriarchal systems have relied heavily upon her (in fact so
much of this ideology is built directly on the back of Eve's transgression) they do not claim her as their own: she is a dissident citizen
of the patriarchy. Those who seek to reinforce these paradigms of
oppressive power-over have denigrated Eve, even while they seem to
desperately need her and value her as proof of their ideologies. And
it is precisely because she stepped beyond the assigned boundaries of
that system that she is denigrated and used in this way.

However, those who desire to abandon such ideologies have at
times also felt the need to abandon Eve. Associating Eve with patriarchy and believing that Eve is too deeply entrenched and complicit
in the patriarchal system to be saved, many have attempted to leave
Eve behind in favor of Lilith. On the other hand, others have tried
to eliminate the patriarchy in the myth by rereading it in a more
female friendly way, still only taking some but not all of Eve and the
Eden story. Paradoxically, many times this is done in defense of those
patriarchal systems themselves, as a way of making staying possible.

However, Eve is more complex than either of these solutions. Eve
is homeopathic and those who have desired our healing from harmful images and ideologies have rejected Eve because they rightfully
sense the illness that is present there. Sadly, this has caused us to
largely miss the medicine she brings us as well: Eve is the first to
transgress, and in her transgression, becomes knowing like the gods.

She does not only offer an image of the submissive helper, obedient
daughter, and compliant mother. She also offers an image of someone
who chooses a different way. Through the very act that caused her to
become a symbol of fallenness and depravity, she finds knowledge
and liberation precisely through what was being buried: the Goddess
and her ways knowing. As Eve transgresses, she follows the wisdom
of serpent and takes in the power of the fruit from the sacred tree.

Rather than rejecting her or denying her lineage in both matriar-
chy and patriarchy, we look at Eve as a whole and allow her to show

us something we need to know when we are also in between, when we also belong to many worlds, when we also feel the searing pain of conflicted loyalties, and when we also live in a muddied and elusive sense of belonging and un-belonging. In this liminal space there can be much shame, tension, and exile. As John O'Donohue put it, "The path you took to get here has washed out; The way forward is still concealed from you."[40] To be truly in between things—loyalties, loves, realities, selves, stories—can be a painful place and also a place of deep alchemical potentiality. Stepping into a liminal space can be especially excruciating if we have been told that there is only one way and that if we leave that one way there will be nothing.

In the kind of creative transgression that we witness in Eve's story, there will be the pain of feeling torn. There will be conflict and doubt. There will even be shame as the favored narratives and values cast judgment upon our transformation. There will be a sense of exile and *not belonging in the old or the new*. The reality of Eve's liminal status reminds us that sometimes we must reckon with both and stay in the difficult questions, rather than sever without reflection. Not always, but sometimes.

Yes, perhaps there would be less grief, maybe it would be easier, if we could simply sever the Garden from our experience. If we could sever the old ways cleanly. And there are some ways of transgressing that constellate this particular experience and are necessary at times. But the Eve experience does not constellate this kind of energy. In the Eve experience of transgression, there is grief, exile, and deep wrestling. There is sorrow. And there is something about that sorrow that keeps the quester bound to multiple narratives and perspectives. There is something about this liminal kind of suffering that acts as alchemical cauldron as we dissolve and become, over and over. Maybe this is what it means to be born again, and again, and again.

This liminal tension could be a tension between what you think you should feel and what you are actually feeling, between cherished ideologies and lived experiences, between loyalties to old paradigms and new modes of being, between identities and narratives that have served you well and unknown identities and stories that would bring disruption to the established order. To live between cherished places, to suffer torn loyalties, is to live with a chronic and deep ache. It is to live with a vast landscape of vulnerability at the center of every day, at the center of the body. It is a tension that can feel like it will erase you, flatten you until you give in to the nothingness. To live in between loyalties is to bear being misunderstood and unseen. It is to continually choose complexity and love over simple reductionism and protective categories. And sometimes, being in that tension and liminality *for a time* is what makes us large enough for the new life that is emerging.

After that conversation on the track, I left broken hearted. The ache in my body felt like the Grand Canyon. I felt unseen and profoundly misunderstood. Eventually, I was able to go to bed and find sleep that night. And it was just the beginning of this long undoing. I went on, a few months later, to graduate from nursing school and get married a week later. I had just turned twenty-three and, for years, I continued to fall into this place in between. Then and each time since, this in-between place teaches me something about grief.

# A NOTE ON GRIEF

*It never grew easy,*
*but at last I grew peaceful...*
*I lay on the rocks, reaching*
*into the darkness, learning*
*little by little to love*
*our only world.*

**Mary Oliver**[41]

What I have discovered over and over again is that living the questions is much, much harder than living the answers. This shift in my life brought profound loss as what I knew was slowly dissolved, as I waited in the dark, as I let people down, and as I learned how to bear being misunderstood and falsely named. Creative transgression has a way of undoing and unraveling us. Our days becomes like sieves as we watch what we have held dear and our cherished plans slip past us into the unknown.

The way of Nature is circular and inclusive–creation and destruction, doing and undoing, growing and decaying, knowing and unknowing, taking in and letting go, filling and emptying. This is a deep and old wisdom and the more we are initiated into the mysteries or the cycles of death and rebirth, the more we will have opportunity to make peace with our lives, with Life.

And...

I have been reflecting on how this profound truth about our nature can be subtly distorted, thus keeping us from the medicine of its mystery. This happens when we get caught up in the *It all will add up* story. The *What doesn't kill you makes you stronger* story. The *It's okay to lose because you will gain even more* story. On the surface it may seem like we are honoring all the cycles of Nature, but if we look more closely another narrative emerges: we are making it all about the math. This rationale goes like this: the gain will outweigh the loss, and so all will be well.

In some of the most difficult moments of unraveling, I have found myself asking, "Will this be worth it?" In other words, will this difficult choice, will this excruciating loss, will this profound grief, be redeemed by the greater gain it will bring? In those times, I have found this question to be a seductive trap, offering the promise of comfort while stealing my energy and obstructing my access to my knowing. It kept me like a hamster on a wheel, moving too quickly on shifting ground.

What I was really asking was aligned with the story that for everything I lose, I will gain more—which is a popular collective distortion of the mystery of the cycles of death and rebirth. I was looking for the equation to work out as a way of making sense of loss and a way accepting my grief. In these moments, the deep mysteries of death and rebirth become a mental math game. It becomes a constant balancing of the equations, of making things add up in our favor.

But this is the thing: we just don't know.

This may not be the most pleasing perspective, but it is the one I hold. We don't know if it will be worth it, if it will all add up, or if what we lost will be made beautiful by what we gain. It is an impossible question to answer.

What is truer to my lived experience is different. Even when we receive and create beautiful lives after loss and grief, what was lost will never be regained or replaced. We will carry our stories and be re-visited by our grief and feel the absence of what we have lost. The relief comes with realizing that in the midst of loss and grief and difficult choices, it is not our task to turn the loss into gain. But rather to be with all of it and make enough space, eventually, for the sorrowful and the beautiful to live side by side.

This is Nature. The Life/Death/Life cycle does not erase loss and decay. It is big enough to hold all of it. And so are we.

Maybe our task is not to spin grief into gold, but rather to cultivate a way of being that is big enough to hold all of it. Maybe our task is about becoming the kind of person that can hold the loss and grief, and also have eyes to see when the first soft rays of sun appear on the horizon. To become the kind of person that can be warmed by that light when it arrives, with a heart expansive enough to welcome the beauty even as it hosts the sadness.

Deep awareness of the Life/Death/Life cycle does offer a profound medicine and deep hope. It does offer healing as we learn to trust that death and rebirth are in continual motion. Sometimes, the hope of new life arriving on the wind does infuse our days with strength to go on when we are exhausted and weary. And, this is different than feeling like we have to wring enough meaning out of loss and grief until it finally makes sense and is replaced by a new and better life.

May we step off the hamster wheel and put down our calculators. This is not how we weave meaning in our lives. Let us feel each other's deep sighs of relief as we place our feet right where we each stand. Remembering the expansiveness of Nature lives within each of us. Remembering that we can hold the loss, the mistakes, the ways we have hurt ourselves and others, the ways others have hurt us, the sadness, the grief … not because we will work hard enough to spin it all into gold, but because we are brave and tender enough to be here loving our lives. Because little by little we will hold more, see more, love more. Because we will watch the magic of alchemy as our lives are held and moved and shaped by the rhythms of death and rebirth. Not because, as Mary Oliver put it, it will get easier, but because we will grow more peaceful. And, so may it be.

Grief is not the only difficult visitor on this path of creative transgression. As we see in the Eden story, shame will also make appearances as we walk with Eve out of obedience and into our wild knowing, into sovereignty.

# SHAME & STORIES
# FORGED IN HELL

*A life truly lived constantly burns away veils of illusion, burns away what is no longer relevant, gradually reveals our essence, until, at last, we are strong enough to stand in our naked truth.*

**Marion Woodman**[42]

It was a sunny breezy southern California afternoon. We sat down outside; we could see the ocean; we could hear the waves. My husband and I sat to talk to important elders in our lives about our religious and spiritual differences. Our request was simple: *we know we live out our spirituality differently. Even though we are different we also have a meaningful spiritual practice and thoughtful lives. And we are asking you to trust and respect us.*

The words landed and started a fire.

One of them jumped in her seat and, before I knew it, her finger was inches from my face, her anger fierce and unleashed, "Do you believe in Jesus? Do you?" And this was only the beginning.

As I sat, stunned, and didn't answer her questions immediately, she smiled with a certain smugness and slowly folded her hands on her lap, "See," she said with satisfaction, "I knew it. I knew it all along. You should be able to say it right away. Well, now I know for sure so I can keep praying for you."

I sat there for what seemed like an eternity, but was probably thirty minutes, as they recited their litany of accusations. "You will have to be accountable someday for how you raise your child, since you are risking his eternity." Another one chimed in, "You have made all of us uncomfortable for years, like an elephant in every room we are in together. Maybe you are this way (i.e. don't go to church) because of how you were raised."

As this continued, I began to recite my mantra in a barely audible whisper: *this is not love, you can't talk to me like this.*

There were no walls. There were no locked doors. But I stayed there, as they poured their judgment on me. I was in shock. And also, I thought that if I left it would only serve as proof to them of everything they were saying. Part of me thought it would be disrespectful, or that I owed them this. I didn't want to be the one to storm off—it would prove to them that I am *that kind of woman.* I could do this. I could stay.

"You don't know God."

*This is not love.*

"I don't see God in you."

*This is not love.*

"You break our hearts every day."

*This is not love.*

I breathe and say, again, "I do have God in my life, it's just different from your way. And I am asking you to trust me and respect me in that."

"I am talking about the God of the Bible, Vanya. You should be able to tell me right now, what you believe."

*This is not love.*

"It is a different God."

Yes. This we agree on.

I finally stood up shakily. The thing I had wept for most, fought for most, sacrificed for most— spiritual freedom and sovereignty— had been ripped from my body by their accusing hands. And they had spent time out of time enacting violence to this most precious, wounded, and healed place at the center of my life. I thought I would dissolve, turn to water, and run off to join the Great Mother—the ocean only a stone's throw away. But I stood up. They moved to hug me. I stood, frozen, as they hugged me, "We love you," they reassured me tenderly. I stood still.

As we walked up the hill, my body trembled violently.

"We need to go," I said to my husband. "We have to leave."

"No, please," he pleaded. "It will seem like we are storming off. I don't want to rock the boat. Take as much time alone as you need and then re-join us." So, I re-joined the group right away because I knew that if I sat alone in a room I would disappear.

We joined everyone at the beach, like nothing had happened. We left, on schedule, a few hours later. No storming off. No boats rocked. All it took was for me to swallow their shadow whole and then thank them for the meal.

In an effort to find agency and accountability for our own lives, we often ask too much of ourselves. We may force ourselves to stay within in a cruel gaze and expect ourselves to "take care of ourselves" or "not let others make us feel" a certain way. In other words, we have been convinced that we are the problem, or we have convinced ourselves we are the ones strong enough to handle this—we swallow the shadow whole and we smile. No boats rocked. And then we wonder why we are tired, why we are angry, why we lack vitality.

Sometimes shame is a canary in the mine, alerting us to a dangerous situation and letting us know we are no longer safe in this environment. Sometimes shame is rooted in the gaze we are living under, not in our own hearts and bodies. We register it in our hearts and bodies, but if we pay attention closely—learning to respond with curiosity rather than judgment—we will notice that it is coming from the gaze, the environment, the beliefs and feelings around us. The message this kind of shame brings us is, *Get out! You and this environment are no longer compatible!* This is the kind of shame we find in the Eden story.

After the transgression, Eve has changed. She has become knowing. Her eyes have been opened. And Eve hides. She and Adam cower in the bushes when they hear Yahweh walking through the Garden in the cool of the evening. Eve's shame is the loudest testament to her former place as the dutiful one, the good obedient girl. Her shame reveals a few realities: she has changed, part of her still believes or is bound by the old way, and she does not want to lose favor.

While she reaches for the fruit and shatters the form of her prior existence, she is still with Adam and still longs for Yahweh's approval. The shame we read in the myth suggests she is still loyal, at least on some level, to Yahweh and to the familiar way—the paradigm she transgresses. Her shame and desire to hide suggest she struggles with disappointing Yahweh (or at least, she still fears him). Her shame shows us that she still feels named by the old ways and yet she knows that she no longer belongs there.

She can no longer stay and be free. She can no longer stay and be uncovered—to stay in the Garden would be to live covered in fig leaves in a constant state of repentance and penance. It seems that she never intended to leave—she simply must, now that she knows.

Psychologically, this shame calls into question one's very sense of being rather than simply one's behavior. This is an experience where one feels the imperative to transgress beyond the approved boundaries and yet still feels bound and named by the very structures one is leaving. There is not yet an image or a moral justification for what is occurring, and one's sense of identity and fundamental worth is called into question.

The shame here implies a deep shift of identity that is both called forth and required by the transgression. Shame in this situation serves as diagnostic and remedy. That is, the shame shows that a shift in identity has occurred and that this identity is not acceptable to the old paradigms and ruling principles. This shame also offers itself as a remedy when it serves as a spark toward movement into the new ways, when it creates the psychic tension necessary for change.

Shame may serve as a silencing force, but it may also serve as a confrontational and energizing force, one that reverberates with the truth of the situation and demands action: lived experience and deep identity are not congruent with this way of being, this gaze, this environment. When we find ourselves hiding and trembling, we must ask ourselves where we are and what choice this state is pressing us into.

In Eve's transgression, shame serves both as a suppressive force (she hides) and as a transformative force (she is no longer acceptable and cannot deny the shift in identity). Sometimes shame is what brings the full force of the transgression to light and makes change inevitable.

After that experience on the beach, I knew I wasn't safe. But I could not rock the boat. I could not "storm off." So, I stayed, at great cost to myself (and my relationships). But the truth is the boat was already being madly tossed around, the storm was already raging. What was really happening was that it became my job to use all my energies to steady my body against the winds so no one would notice the storm. My job was to believe their words, take on their names, and remain under their gaze. My job was to absorb. My job was to feel shame—shame that would keep me silent and give them voice. Shame that would keep me wrong and them right. Shame that would keep me bad and them good. Shame that would make me hide. However, this shame was both suppressive and explosive, in that it broke the spell of complicity and offered me the energy I needed to, eventually, transgress that story and that role.

For much of my life I have been so good at naming the cost of transgression—the cost of letting go, of being good and of being obedient to what is expected of me. I think many of us are experts at naming the cost of disrupting the status quo, describing in detail how everyone else will be hurt, inconvenienced, annoyed, or even betrayed. Often the effect of our reaching for what we long for on the partners, the parents, the children, the dogs, and the cat is an easily told tale. And yet, it is often much more difficult to name the cost of not reaching, the cost of remaining in the status quo, the cost of staying good. I have slowly been learning how to name the harm and betrayal to my own life when I choose to ignore what my body, intuition, and instincts are telling me. I have experienced the devastating cost of disobedience, and sometimes the cost is indeed very high. But the cost of choosing to ignore my true questions, vision, longing, and knowing is simply no longer tolerable to me.

For many of us, we have been indoctrinated to take on the shadows around us, telling stories like: *We can do this. We are strong. Everyone else is fine now, so it's okay. I will take this rather that confront it. I will live in this story because if I don't all hell will break loose.* In my experience, sometimes stories that serve as protective vessels for containing some kind of hell have been forged and are sustained in some kind of hell. The storm is already raging; the boat is already tipping over. Sometimes we need to let the energy we have been absorbing for everyone else in order to keep the boat steady, be the energy that helps us unleash hell.

The confrontation with a cruel gaze kept me still for a few hours, but then it made it impossible for me to do nothing. I had already felt the cruel gaze and all the shame it planted in my body, it had already been there alerting me to the danger, but it was cloaked in gentle politeness. So, I accepted the burden because I could not prove it. In other words, my own experience—the messages and sufferings of my heart, soul, and body—were not enough evidence. But as I sat there, watching what had been living under the surface be unearthed and materialize around me, I had to make a choice. I could continue to internalize this shame and continue to be harmonious to this system at great cost to myself, or I could find a way to no longer comply with that system. The force of it made me choose: would I stay here and be continually shamed by this gaze or would I transgress?

The curse became blessing.

The shame became energy because it was exceedingly clear that in order to remain harmonious here, I would have to hide, I would have to be silent, I would have to smile and comply. *I would have to live covered in fig leaves.* That was the choice. No amount of inner work and soul searching were going to change the reality of the cruel gaze.

I would never expect any other tender creature to thrive under cruel conditions where shame and shunning are the weapons and anesthetics of choice, why would I expect that from myself? Why would you expect that from yourself?

This experience brings up another aspect of transgression out of the shoulds that I have experienced many times: moving beyond the shoulds and into your wild knowing will emphasize any fundamentalist attitudes within your own psyche and in the world around you. This is something to be aware of because, like I mentioned above, these narratives can be like binding curses. One of the lies we are told in fundamentalist ideologies is that if we leave the approved and favored paradigm there will be a vast landscape of nothingness. A wasteland. There will be nothing: no meaning, no sacredness, no community, no belonging, no blessing. This is a story that serves as a powerful curse that binds us and keeps us from stepping into the largeness before us and within us.

# A NOTE ON FUNDAMENTALISM

*Stepping into largeness will require that we discern our
personal authority – rather than the authority of others
or the authority of our internalized admonitions – and
live this inner authority with risk and boldness.*

**James Hollis**[43]

Fundamentalism is always religious but is not always about a religion. It is religious because it is always rooted in the fervent realms of the psyche that deal with truth, passion, attitude, and belief. One can have a fundamentalist attitude about anything. In the way I understand it, fundamentalism is to confuse the way we know, experience, and seek something with the something itself. It is to conflate the *way* we know, with *what* we know.

In a religious setting this could mean that someone who meaningfully experiences the numinous realm of the sacred through a particular religious image or ideology—such as Jesus, Buddha, salvation, nirvana or church—might then believe that those images and ideologies are themselves the meaning and the numinous realm, rather than portals that point us toward something ineffable. In this perspective, to lose those images and ideologies would be to lose meaning and the numinous realm themselves. Or someone might believe the only way to find belonging is to be successful in business, or that to find safety one must accumulate wealth. A fundamentalist attitude causes what they are knowing or trying to know, i.e., belonging and safety, to be confused with how they are experiencing those things, i.e., through business and wealth. And so, if a business fails or money is lost, a person with this fundamentalist posture might believe they have lost belonging and safety themselves, rather than one of the many ways of knowing them. In fundamentalism, the many ways become the One Way, as the bridges become the destinations, as portals become closed doors. The way someone is experiencing (or trying to experience) something is not the something itself, and to conflate the two is to be trapped in fundamentalism.

What if images, like everything in Nature, also are caught up in the continual cycles of death and rebirth? What if the images must always die and go to seed, allowing new images to emerge? What if each time an archetypal image withers and falls away, we are invited to wait for new images that will once again point us toward the archetype itself? What if this continual spiral of ascent and descent takes us deeper with and deeper into meaning and sacred belonging? What if the death of an ideology, value, image, or worldview is the way we get closer to those very things we thought were lost?

It is terrifying when what is most precious to us becomes a static thing that can easily be threatened, broken, or taken—like a mighty wind caught in a glass vial, the Wild Uncontrollable imagined as a fragile thing cupped in our small hands. Radiant portals into the realm of the unknowable become walls as we try to keep the mysteries contained in too-small rooms. And if we believe that without those rooms, we will lose relationship with meaning, belonging, love, or purpose, we will indeed be willing to fight to the death to protect those rooms. Fundamentalism and militant attitudes walk hand in hand.

If your parents, partners, or community of friends believes there is only one way to be human that is satisfying (whether that is about a particular religion, career, family structure, relationship style, sexual identity or orientation... we could go on) the resistance and fear will be great. They will not only be fighting for that religion, career, or lifestyle, but also for meaning, salvation, purpose, and happiness. They have conflated these archetypal experiences (or the ways they believed and hoped they would experience these things) with the archetypes themselves, the way they are knowing with what they are knowing. There is no easy way through. But we start with looking and naming.

This lie of fundamentalism—that if you leave this One Way you will have nothing and that you will live in a wasteland with no meaning or belonging—must be named and not forgotten. This lie can keep you in a too-small paradise, believing you must forgo what you sense and see for the sake of false safety.

May this curse be banished over and over again as we choose to follow our knowing beyond the boundaries of our indoctrination to be good. When all we can see is ruin and all we can feel is desolation, may the seeds buried in our lives begin to glow with warmth and promise. When it seems like there is only one story and one way, may we hear the distant echoes of our ancestors and allies reminding us that there are many stories and many ways. From the interwoven intricacy of a spider web to the complexity of how galaxies reach for one another, may we witness and be reminded of the beautiful multiplicity and interconnection of Nature and that, truly, we can never fall out of what we are made of. We are made of earth and stardust; our belonging is deep and expansive and irrevocable.

We will need to remember this truth because the question of belonging and unbelonging will inevitably arise as we learn to step into truer and deeper ways of being in the world. One of the sacrifices involved in this kind of transgression is this: to risk our belonging in the old places. In my experience, the walk toward truer belonging usually involves painful periods of unbelonging. Belonging and unbelonging also walk hand in hand.

# (UN)BELONGING & BELONGING

*The world needs your rebellion and the true song of
your exile. In what has been banned from your life,
you find a medicine to heal all that has been kept from
our world... The world needs your unbelonging.*

**Toko-pa Turner**[44]

In the religious community I grew up in we shared land, money,
food, and most importantly, purpose and belief. I loved belonging to
a larger community and I still miss it. Sometimes I am still confound-
ed by the way life here in the United States can be so isolated. I miss
the feeling of living alongside others in that kind of community. I remember when I was a child feeling so much anxiety when we would
leave to go on a vacation. Just us! Out in the world! The community
offered me a sense of shelter and safety. And I still seek to craft a life
that is embedded in the shelter of community and resist that strong
current of modern life to carve out isolated and parallel lives.

But I didn't only know the glory of belonging. I also knew its
shadow. Everything casts a shadow. When the light of consciousness
touches something, a shadow is created too. Belonging is no different.
Sometimes the shadow is natural, and we live it in the form of holy
sacrifices in the name of what we love. Sometimes the shadow is long
and profound, and we live it in the form of unconscious possession. In
my case, the glory of belonging to this community was truly brilliant,
and the shadow was long and deep. The cost of belonging was high.

In order to belong and find favor, I had to obey. I had to believe
the things I was told. I had to behave in the way I was taught to

behave. I had to think the right thoughts and feel the right feelings. I had to mirror my environment in a way that affirmed it. I wonder if this is true for most of us in our experiences of belonging when we are young, just in varying degrees of constriction or freedom.

Sometimes we speak about belonging as if it were a simple or static thing. But belonging is complex. True and loving belonging is one of the most meaningful and foundational experiences in Nature. And yet, when belonging becomes static and divorced from care and reverence for the other, it can quickly become a deadening force. The sheltering walls of belonging can become imprisoning walls when belonging is used as weapon.

Belonging is used as weapon when it says *obey or be exiled, comply or be disowned.* Perhaps, when belonging is a dead thing—unchanging and cold—it becomes something else. When we find ourselves in this kind of story, it is a good time to wonder about this belonging and who it is serving. What does your longing tell you? What does your wild knowing whisper to you in the quiet moments? How does this belonging make you feel, and what does the light of this belonging cast into the shadow? As we ask these questions, it is very helpful to choose curiosity over judgment. Sometimes we need to stay in constrictive or false belonging for a time, until we are ready to lose what has sheltered us (even if poorly). Sometimes we are still gathering what we will need for our journey to a deeper and truer belonging—a journey that will almost always include painful times of sacred unbelonging. We go with tenderness, doing our best not to lie to ourselves and to choose our sacrifices wisely, patiently, and bravely.

The kind of belonging I long for is not about ownership or control. It is belonging as being a part of. Belonging not as property but as kin. Belonging through inclusion, not ownership. Belonging through relationship, not hierarchy. This kind of belonging, because it is not dead but is alive, vibrant, and dynamic, will inevitably include experiences of unbelonging.

When, finally, all my resources had been spent paying the too-high price of belonging and I had borrowed as much as I could from willpower and effort, I collapsed. After that Tuesday on the lawn chair, I didn't get out of bed the next day. Over the next years of deep inner conflict and debilitating depression, I slipped out of the belonging I had treasured so much and wandered into a time of unbelonging. It was deeply painful as I didn't know what ideas, beliefs, hopes, communities, or places to tether myself to. I didn't know what my name was anymore. I had to wander, wrestle, weep, and wait. This was a time of sacred unbelonging. Sacred unbelonging meets us when we transgress the boundaries of previous (old and/or false) belonging as the longing for truer lives stirs and moves us.

The *Malleus Maleficarum*, also known as *The Witches' Hammer*, was one of the most influential books during the Middle Ages. In fact, at the time of its publication in the late fifteenth century, its popularity was second only to the Judeo-Christian Bible, and it was endorsed by the Catholic Church. In this text, the authors, two priests named Kramer and Sprenger, detailed the depravation of witches, explained tests to identify witches, and prescribed the appropriate punishment (most often death) for witches. In a poignant section on why most witches are female, Kramer and Sprenger looked to Eve to prove the inherent inferiority and debasement of the female sex, as well as to emphasize women's dangerous powers of sexuality and seduction, "For it is true that in the Old Testament the Scriptures have much that is evil to say about women, and this because of the first temptress, Eve, and her imitators."[45] Here we witness Eve being used as the foundational justification of the inferiority and, therefore, subjugation of women. But this view and use of Eve did not stop in the construction of ideologies. It has, over and over again, been metabolized into violent action.

For example, this view of Eve embraced in *Malleus Maleficarum* was closely linked with the justification for not only the subjugation of females, but also for the murder of females. It is estimated that during the time of the witch-hunts, also called the Burning Times, thousands of people, mostly women, were killed—there are varying estimates regarding the exact number because, as is most often the case in systems of oppression, the suffering, the stories, and the names of those oppressed are nearly erased. Nearly. These horrific acts of violence and murder stand in powerful opposition to the common opinion that our ancient myths do not matter or have practical and political significance. Everything we do, starts with a myth living through us.

In the *Malleus Maleficarum*, the authors claimed that the top three vices of female witches are "infidelity, ambition, and lust."[46] This little line, in my view, is at the heart of this rhetoric. Eve, and her "imitators," i.e. all females, are evil if they belong to themselves: if they show faithfulness to their own desire and lives above their faithfulness to their duties to family and religion, if they show personal drive toward their own visions, and if they express sexual desire that is rooted in their own bodies and imagination, they will be feared and condemned. They will be punished and killed. The mandate to be obedient and to exist for the external expectations and needs of others is very old indeed. Our indoctrination to never belong to ourselves is not a footnote in our history: it is foundational. It is visceral. It lives in our cellular memory.

What would happen in the world if we belonged to ourselves?

That liminal space where we suddenly un-belong to what we have belonged to, is an invitation for us to know our deepest self-belonging. When there is nothing left to trust, we have to ask if we will trust ourselves. Will we trust our longing, our intuition, our bodies, our knowing? During these times, our invisible roots, our hollow threads, are not tethered to something out there, external, but to the mystery of our own lives. It might be precisely this unbelonging that presses us irrevocably into our deepest self-belonging. Perhaps it is when we finally don't belong to anyone, anything, or any place that we finally find the freedom to belong to ourselves. Perhaps when there is nothing external left to hold on to, we finally hold on to our wild souls. In this way we may learn how to be the deepest sources of our own permission, worth, and nourishment.

# SELF-BELONGING

*The swan doesn't cure his awkwardness by beating himself on the back, by moving faster, or by trying to organize himself better. He does it by moving toward the elemental water, where he belongs. It is the simple contact with the water that gives him grace and presence. You only have to touch the elemental waters in your own life, and it will transform everything.*

**David Whyte**[47]

Growing up, I knew what it meant to be a good girl. I would be serene, helpful, compliant, and kind. I would not question. I would serve. I would not be too strong, but nor would I need too much. When I was much older, I would be sexual enough to please my husband (the possibility that I would not have a husband or that I would have a wife were never even mentioned) but not sexual enough to make other men lust. And I would certainly not be sexual enough to have sexual autonomy and agency—I would never belong to myself. I would be religiously devout, but I would not be spiritual enough to be my own spiritual authority, my own high priestess—I would never belong to myself. I would love God the Father above all else. I would belong to him via my father for a while and then, via another man when my father gave me away (here we are, centuries later, still reenacting the Eden story: Woman given to Man by the Father, the Mother unwritten from the story). I would never belong to myself.

After thirteen years in Seattle, I moved out of my little house and out of the city. I moved an hour north of Seattle onto five acres of land at the foot of a mountain on the edge of the sea—the ocean on the west side of the mountain and our small homestead on the east side of the mountain. This mountain has been logged for years (and sadly, has been named after the family that logged it for decades; I am still waiting to learn its true name). Many of the old cedars are gone and have been replaced by alders, cottonwoods, pines, maples, and lots of berry bushes. But still, on this little piece of land where I live, many cedars remain. Right in front of my house stand three towering cedars, right on the edge of a slope down to the small year-round creek. They are sentinels. They are memory keepers. They are still here and their presence over the land is formidable. I love them—one in particular. She has a thick truck that splits into two and reaches up into the skies.

The ease of trees, even as they carry so much memory and communal responsibility, draws me in. Their connections reach vertically through space and horizontally through time. This cedar has lived through much, and as I make a new life in her shade, in the shadow of the mountain, I often place my hand on her body and ask her to teach me to be like her: slow and true. Her roots reach for water and communion below, and her branches reach up toward the light and air. By her side, I sense that strange mixture of heaviness and ease that come with initiated cronehood. With my palm on her thick trunk, I imagine into her long life here on this land and I ask this land to welcome my family, I promise to honor the life and death of the land, to honor the ancestors of this land. I let myself feel the conflict and sorrow of living on occupied land, and I humble myself before the Elders, open handed and open hearted. As my hand becomes sticky with sap, I feel the strength of her body and imagine deep with her, down into her roots, down into her source, down into her home—where she came from and to where she will return.

This Mother Cedar rises from the life of all things like a song of praise and for a time sings her melody, and one day will return to where she came from. In her long life, she would have taken up space in the shadow of this mountain, having been embedded in the community of the forest she would have risen to be one of the elders of this place, and then returned to the ground and air in a final act of communion as her body became sustenance and nourishment for the community of all things—her body returning to bodies, becoming Body once more. This is also our story. Though our roots are invisible, they are no less real.

Our self-belonging is inextricably bound to our greater belonging to each other and to this Earth, to these cyclical mysteries of death and rebirth. Our self-belonging has to do with our permission and freedom—spiritual, emotional, physical, sexual, cultural, religious, socio-political—to find our own song of praise, unique and true. To take up that space and live wholeheartedly from the wildness that comes from knowing and honoring our nature, and then when the time comes, to return.

The deeper we follow our self-belonging, the more we may find our belonging in the life of all things. This is the paradox. Like Mother Cedar, our roots make us stronger in our own identity and place, and also make us more intricately connected to everything else. If we are rooted in ourselves, we are rooted in everything else. The boundaries between inner and outer, between the world in here and the world out there, fade away.

If we are made of this Earth and hold the mysteries of Nature in these small temples, when we move inward, we find the world and when we move outward, we find ourselves. Where our roots reach for water and nourishment, naming us and holding us up, they also find our belonging and our connection to the world. Self-belonging is about permission to live from the nourishment, communion, and knowing that travel up through our roots, manifesting as our outward expressions of life. It is not about the neurotic idea of disconnected individualism, rugged and unbound. It is not about selfishness, unrelatedness, or greed. It is about wildness—embedded, connected, and free. This is the kind of wild belonging Cedar embodies.

To be wild means to know what you are, what you are made of, and to live from that place without shame. To be domesticated, on the other hand, is to live by the rules of another. Remember, seeds? They can wait so long until the time is right. And then, in a fury of fate the seed breaks open and possibility become incarnated. As we surrender to the fates hidden within the seeds of our lives and befriend what we are becoming, we move toward our belonging to the wild—within and without. In the breaking open, what we thought to be the ending becomes the beginning.

Belonging ourselves to the wild within and without is deep homecoming and can also involve painful exile from what was false or from what we have outgrown. Leaving domestication can be an exceedingly painful experience and a true initiation. This initiation often catapults into that time of sacred unbelonging. May we recognize the liminal spaces of unbelonging as invitations into a deeper, truer, and wilder self-belonging.

# THE GOOD ENOUGH PARADISE

*I tried to live small.*
*I took a narrow bed.*
*I held my elbows to my sides...*
*Yet see how I spread out and I cannot help it.*

**Naomi Replansky**[48]

I am in an underground room, maybe an abandoned subway station. It has the eerie feeling of having been emptied and left in a hurry, trash rustling in the stale breeze from the empty tunnels. One lone red chair haphazardly taking up space in the middle of the room. In all this, the beautiful aqua blue tile floors stand out—they are beautiful. I am watching this scene with a figure beside me, male and hooded. "This is your work, make this space beautiful," he says as he moves his arm in a sweeping gesture across the abandoned room. I begin to imagine that task and all I could do to make this underground room beautiful. I have ideas.

When I woke from this dream, I realized that dread had made a home in the pit of my stomach. I knew this dream was more than it appeared to be, but I didn't understand it at first. As I moved closer to the dream, over time, I began to understand the dangers I felt in the dream: the danger of being seduced into believing that what is keeping me small and slowly stealing away my life, is beautiful. The danger of a good-enough paradise.

In the little city-house I used to live in, there was a tree right outside my bedroom window. This tree had a vine wrapped around its trunk and branches, and in the winter when the tree lost all of its leaves, the vine was the most beautiful thing on the tree. When everything seemed dead, this vine was green and growing. It was difficult to live in a big city with little yard space and I loved the green outside my window through the long gray winters of Seattle. I knew, though. I knew that the vine, although it appeared to be one of the most vibrant parts of this tree, was in truth stealing its life. I knew that eventually it would kill the tree that I loved. I knew that it seemed to embrace and adorn the very thing that it was stealing from. I knew all of this, and yet the thought of cutting it down was painful—it was so beautiful, and it brought me comfort in the concrete winter harshness of city life. I told myself eventually we would cut it down, but just not yet.

The dream was showing me the seduction of the vine. The hooded figure was trying to convince me it would be beautiful to spend my life fulfilling the fate of making this abandoned underground room beautiful, even as I sensed the vibrant wild hum of life just above.

Sometimes what we think beautiful and life giving is actually the thing that is siphoning away our life. The dream showed me that what was at risk was my life, my largeness. I could have spent my life toiling to obey the mandate, and I know I would have made the best of it—*like a good girl always does*. I could have spent my life in a too-small paradise.

Our birthright is to be wild, not to live in too-small cages we are taught to call paradise. We have been taught that these cages are safe, and it is so hard to let go of safety. But here is the thing, a lot of times we think something is safe because it is approved. Those are not the same thing. Favor and safety must not be confused. This is Eve's paradise: to be seduced with illusions of safety and comfort by what is secretly colluding toward our disappearance. It seems safe to obey. It seems safe to not speak up, not to tell our stories, not to listen to our bodies, not to heed the truths of our hearts. All it costs us is our knowing and our sovereignty. But as we begin to trust our bodies, honor our hunger, and reach for what we desire, our eyes may be opened and we may realize that what has promised us safety is, in fact, harming us. We may awaken to the reality that what we call good-enough or even paradise, is stealing away our lives.

In Eve's paradise, she is cared for and lives in favor, as long as she stays away from one thing: knowing. She is promised safety and security in exchange for obedience. She lives in a beautiful Garden and enjoys a protected existence. On the surface she seems to want for nothing. However, she experiences a longing for more. She experiences curiosity and desire. Eve suffers the incongruent stories of a good-enough paradise. Her longing is not congruent with the story that she has everything she could need or desire. Her longing challenges the serenity of the collective perception and outward situation. It has to do with more hidden truths, secret knowing, and unprovable needs.

Eve exists at the threshold between what someone believes they should think and feel about their lives and what they actually experience. Even though the story on the surface of the paradisaical life is that all should be well, the lived experience is one of longing and desire, as the inner call for more becomes louder and the transgressive energy begins to gain strength and shape. How often I have heard someone, including myself, express a deep longing or sorrow followed by a quick, *but it's all in my head* or *I feel discontent but I should be grateful* or *I don't know what's wrong with me, someone else would do anything to have what I have* and other similar platitudes that serve to silence the soul and to banish our disruptive longings. If you find yourself saying these things, it is a good time for curiosity. You may be living in a too-small life and trying to call it paradise. If so, Eve offers herself as a powerful guide out of that paradise and into sovereignty.

Eve may show up in the life of someone who does the right thing, follows the rules, and lives a stable (obedient) life, and yet feels a deep stirring to reach beyond the boundaries of that prescribed life. At this threshold, Eve rises as an energy that enables someone to tell the truth of lived experience, even if it goes against cherished ideologies and approved collective narratives. Eve lives in the paradise of the good-enough, one thing on the surface but another story running through. But remember, Eve transgresses and becomes like the gods, knowing and sovereign.

Living in this web of incongruent narratives can be so strange and difficult. It can feel like living in a house of mirrors, where it can be so hard to discern what is real. When you find yourself living a story no one but you knows or believes, you may become caught between two realities: the one you are being asked to live on the surface and the one you are actually experiencing. It can feel like living in a fog, not knowing what or who to trust. On the outside things may seem solid and good, but an unrest rages below the surface telling a different story. When there is peace and *everything someone could want* on the outside but no depth and little satisfaction, a difficult choice must eventually be made. Which story will be trusted?

When the bargains and stories we have made in our lives are no longer acceptable, the reckoning can be devastating at first. The eruption of these stories sometimes burns us, wounds us, and hopefully eventually liberates us to live more freely and more truly. During these times, it is exceedingly valuable to listen to the stories the body and the heart are telling. They are a compass within that house of mirrors, pointing us toward what is most real in our lives.

I have experienced this truth many times. During times when I have been waking up to the realities of my own incongruent narratives and too-small paradises, but having difficulty bringing those stories into the world, my heart and body have spoken their truths— incessantly and relentlessly. Even, and especially, when I have been busy doing mental gymnastics, trying to land in the right place where my heart would feel what the favored story recommended, what I thought I should feel and wanted to feel. Even as the gravitational streams that shaped my outward life continually pulled me back into the favored story (as the favored stories usually do), attempting to cover up the emerging truths, my heart and body have been faithful in their refusal to lie. *The heart and body are wildly unruly creatures.* We may try to look away, to ignore, to push underground our longing and our unrest but our hearts and bodies become the gatekeepers of our truer stories, alerting us to the danger of abandoning ourselves.

For some folks it is not yet physically safe to transgress the assigned stories. Depending on geography, culture, religion, gender, sexual orientation, skin color, economic circumstance, and domestic situation, silence may be the only option for now. This is the cunning of the knower. Open eyed cunning. For those of us who have the privilege to transgress the expectations imposed upon us without serious physical danger, let us remember our kin. Let us all have open eyes and fierce love as we remember: we belong to each other. Let us show our belonging through our actions, votes, conversations, and spending. Let us show our belonging to each other through how we live and love.

# BOOK THREE:
## EVE'S WAYS OF KNOWING

*Let us remember ourselves back to the wild soul. Let us sing her
flesh back onto our bones. Shed any false coats we have been
given. Don the true coat of powerful instinct and knowing.*

*Infiltrate psychic lands that once belonged to us.*

*Unfurl the bandages, ready the medicine. Let us return now, wild
women howling, laughing, singing to The One who loves us so.*

**Clarissa Pinkola Estés** [49]

# WIT & WITCH

*Those singled out as witches were frequently characterized
by the fact that they had or were believed to have power
arising from a particular kind of knowledge, as in the
case of 'wise women' who knew the curative powers of
herbs and to whom people went for counsel and help...
the word 'witch' is allied with 'wit,' basically to know.*

**Mary Daly**[50]

The majority of Brazil identifies as Catholic. When Brazil was colonized by Portugal in the sixteenth century, the Portuguese brought with them Roman Catholicism and were followed by European Jesuit missionaries. African religions were also introduced to Brazil through the African slave trade. And, of course before any of these arrivals, the indigenous religions of that land shaped the spiritual and religious atmosphere.

In my rural neighborhood in southeastern Brazil it was not uncommon to see the remnants of *Macumbaria* rituals on the side of the road, remnants like dead chickens, bowls, and candle stubs. The term *Macumba* is a lot like the term pagan—it is used by those in power or by the monotheisms to describe anyone who is not them. In other words, it conflates many different views and religions into one Other, to be more specific, one Evil Other. In the case of Macumba, it refers mostly to the African religions that were introduced to Brazil with the African diaspora. As has often been the case, religions associated with people of color and with women have been systematically linked to evil. These religions have often been simply called 'occult' or 'witchcraft,' relying heavily on the unquestioned assumption that witches, who are mostly female, are evil. Again, remember the *Malleus Maleficarum* and its connection to the Catholic Church.

Once a year at a nearby lake, hundreds of seekers would gather to celebrate the festival of Iemanjá, the Goddess of the seas. Women dressed in large white dresses would gather in and around white tents and seekers and worshippers would gather to make offerings and ask for blessings. The Christian missionaries also showed up to pray against the occult and to try to save the lost souls. One year when I was about thirteen years old, I was among these missionaries.

I had seen many festivals like this. I was familiar with spiritism and the healers dressed in white. Large circles were formed with drumming, trance, blessings, dancing, and channeling. I had been taught to fear these rituals, to see these seekers and worshippers as lost souls walking into the devil's den. And I genuinely cared. On this night, as I wove my way through the crowds, I saw a young woman I knew from my neighborhood. I went to her and I could tell she was desperate for what she was seeking here. She was desperate for the blessings this woman in a white dress was about to invoke. I was deeply moved and concerned. Since I believed she was in danger, I begged her to not do this. I begged her to seek blessing from the Christian God instead. She looked me in the eyes and calmly and sadly said no and went on to receive her blessing.

As I have walked into my own path and expanded my understanding, I have thought of that moment many times. My heart aches at how I may have hurt this young woman. So much was lost to me. So much I could have seen and learned but didn't. So much care I could have offered but didn't know how. I was trying to love but was giving a love that didn't make sense, and, I am sure now, did not feel like love.

The Christianity I grew up in was charismatic, full of passion and dancing and speaking in tongues. Full of miracles, demons, and angels. Of course, it was also deeply influenced by the animism running just below the Catholic surface of Brazil. In our meetings we would dance and sing. People would prophesy and engage in oracular knowing. Worshipers would be filled with the spirit and go into altered states of consciousness.

Isn't it interesting how closely this resembles the scene at the lake? However, one was imagined as occult and one as holy. The primary difference was the source. Mary Daly wrote, "The witch's knowledge has always been that of one who foretells…when this is done in the name of one of the established religions it is called prophecy, but when divination is done in the name of a pagan god it is called 'mere' witchcraft."[51] My guess is that there was benevolence and malevolence swirling in both places and, as always, careful discernment is required. But instead I was taught that one was good because it was in the name of the Christian male white God and his prophets, and one was bad because it was not. It was the Evil Other.

When the goddesses were suppressed during the Great Reversal, so were the ways of knowing associated with their traditions. Any knowing that came from sources other than the emerging monotheisms and their priests and prophets was considered evil and was violently silenced—and in many ways, it still is. Consider our reactions to these pairs of words: prophet and prophetess, priest and priestess, God and Goddess, wizard and witch. Again, when divination has been done in the name of the established religions (and the men who point us to a god made in their own image), they have been considered holy, while prophetesses were being systematically eliminated.

In her powerful book, *When God Was a Woman*, Merlin Stone notes the possible significance in the fact that the Hebrew word *zonah* is sometimes translated as "prostitute" and other times as "prophetess."[52] In this muddied association, the knowing of the prophetess becomes entangled with the social marginalization of the sex worker. Just as Eve's knowing and sovereignty were entangled with ideas around evil sexuality and depraved body, so here we witness feminine and female knowing become entangled with ostracized female bodies and illicit sex.

Another illustration of this kind of muddied (and strategic association) is the serpent. The serpent, a complex symbol, was primarily associated with wisdom, divination, and prophecy.[53] Scholars have suggested that the venom of the cobra itself could have been used as medium for the prophetesses of the Goddess to enact their divination and foretelling.[54] In the Eden story, the knowing of the serpent—an ancient source of wisdom associated with the Goddess and her priestesses—became the source of sin and death.

When one way of knowing was elevated, other ways of knowing were suppressed. Traditionally, the Western worldview is a paradigm that values literalism, singularity, and rationality. The more literal and material something is, the more real it is considered. The more singular and unchanging something is, the more it is validated as true. The more linear and rational something is, the higher its position in the hierarchy of valid knowledge. Simultaneously, the fluid, multiple, non-rational, and metaphoric are cast into the shadows. Rather than interconnection, interdependence, and reciprocity that are inherent in our reality, we are forced to live within rigid hierarchical systems that convince us that separateness, hierarchy, and standardization are our truest nature. These systems and ideologies rely heavily on the control of approved knowledge and approved ways of knowing. It is not coincidental that so many of the ways of knowing that don't support compliance with the singular elevated ideology are suppressed.

The shadows of the Eden story reveal ways of knowing that were exiled when other ways of knowing were elevated. In Eve's transgression, wandering, pleasure, longing, desire, body, and more-than-human nature emerge as powerful ways of knowing. Jung pointed out the difficulty of creating meaningful dialogue between what is known and what is unknown while remaining rigidly in the old ways of knowing.[55] For Jung, the alchemy of individuation happens as our consciousness engages in transformative relationship with the unconscious, both personal and collective. The challenge is that our consciousness is accustomed to specific ways of knowing. Like streams carved into the land guiding the water to the same place over and over, so too our ways of knowing can become etched in our consciousness, continually guiding us to where we have already been. Finding new ways of knowing opens up possibilities for us to be led to new knowledge and vast unexplored inner landscapes. Part of the work of creating new consciousness is transgressing and reaching beyond old ways of knowing and their approved sources.

We transgress the hierarchy of The One and, again, invite the many. It all belongs. The question becomes not which one is right or wrong, but which one is called for now. In expanding our ways of knowing, allowing more and more to belong, we are transgressing beyond the approved and favored sources of knowing that have exiled so many beautiful voices, and ultimately calling ourselves—our own wild nature—powerful and trustworthy sources of knowing.

# WANDERING & COAGULATIO

*Here at the beginning, the maiden becomes a wanderer, and this in and of itself is a resurrection into a new life, and a death in the old.*

**Clarissa Pinkola Estés** [56]

Eve's transgression has a wandering quality to it. That is, there is no indication that she set out with a goal or a particular destination in mind. She does not seem pulled forward by transcendent or high goals reached through willful effort. Eve is in the Garden, perhaps walking as the myth suggests they often do, and she comes across the serpent. She does not envision where she wants to end up and plan in order to get there. It is as if the transgression happens without premeditation. She seems to simply go from one intuitive and instinctual impulse to the next.

Not all mythic transgressions have this quality. Ariadne's transgression, for example, happens in a different way. When Ariadne falls in love with Theseus and wants to leave her father's kingdom, she consults Daedalus and makes a carefully thought out plan: the ball of thread that eventually leads Theseus out of the maze after slaying the Minotaur, thus offering Ariadne a way out of King Minos' kingdom and into her own adventures.

Psyche is another mythic figure that transgresses. She is ordered never to look at her lover's face. She loves him and, eventually, she is no longer satisfied with making love in the dark and must see him. So, she plans and prepares. She gathers what she thinks she needs: an oil lamp and a knife. After they make love in the dark and after he falls asleep, she approaches him and lifts the lamp with one hand, while the other holds the knife. She sees her lover's face for the first time, and realizes he is the god Eros. For Psyche too, the transgression is just the beginning of her adventures.

It is interesting that the transgression in all of these mythic images lead to descent, exile, and eventually, the realm of the sacred. After being abandoned by Theseus, Ariadne marries the god Dionysus. After suicidal and treacherous tasks, Psyche returns with Eros to Olympus, and after listening to the serpent and eating the forbidden fruit Eve becomes like the gods. Transgression in all of these instances leads to knowing and sovereignty. While they are all ignited by desire, they show us different ways of enacting the transgression. Psyche and Ariadne both plan and prepare. Eve walks and wanders. Ariadne consults experts. Eve looks and listens. Psyche waits for the dark. Eve feeds the immediacy of hunger. This sensual and wandering way are an important aspect of Eve's way of transgression and knowing. Although wandering is not highly valued in patriarchal ways of being, here it emerges as a powerful way of knowing that acts like the spark that ignites the transgression.

To wander is to walk aimlessly, leisurely, without a specific outcome or destination. To wander effectively one must follow whims, curiosity, and sometimes signs and omens beckoning us to turn into that one market street or to brave into the territory of that forbidden thought or unknown emotion. Wandering can be joyful and playful. Wandering can be exhausted and desperate. Wandering happens when we commit to no path in order to see where the moment takes us. Wandering also happens when what we had planned on, looked to, and hoped for falls through and we are left with no direction, no purpose, and no goal. When life as we have known it ends, we are often sent off to wander.

When we don't even know what to hope for, it is a good time to wander, lest we hope for the wrong thing. I think of T.S. Eliot's words: "I said to my soul, be still, and wait without hope. For hope would be hope for the wrong thing; wait without love. For love would be love of the wrong thing; there is yet faith. But the faith and the love and the hope are all in the waiting."[57] Wandering offers the wanderer the space to move, explore, notice, and experience without a final destination or ideal image. The liminal space wandering creates makes room for something new to emerge. The paradox is that when wandering offers itself as a way of being with the unknown, it becomes a powerful way of knowing. In many myths, wandering is essential. Often, without wandering, the adventurer would have never found her treasure.

After that Tuesday on the lawn chair, I continued to lose my direction. I had oriented my whole life around this idea, this love, this future serving this God. And now, I didn't know what to hope for or envision. It felt like there would be nothing. I had no imagination for the moment, much less an idea of a future destination. So, I wandered for many years.

For me this looked like repeatedly quitting my stable job as a nurse to work at cafés and play live music. It looked like moving a lot. It looked like profound depression. The loss kept unfolding and all I could do was wait without hope. All I could do was wait without faith. Still I had a sense of an unnamed longing that was my only compass. During that time the longing took the shape of writing music and singing. I followed it. I held on to it. During this time, I was also deeply nourished by true friendship and the magic of books.

In alchemy, the process of one thing becoming another is understood in stages. One of the primary and inevitable stages of transformation is the *dissolutio*. This is when the *prima materia*, the raw material, is dissolved into formlessness. During this time of wandering, I felt formless. This is the gift and truth of wandering: we don't have to know anything but the next breath, the next moment, the next step. It is protective, keeping us from choosing a path before we know who we are becoming or where we are going. But then, at some point during the alchemical process *coagulatio*, coagulation, begins. The formlessness begins to take form. One cell at a time, bonds are made, and shapes emerge. I have never found a more apt image for what this season felt like, both the dissolution and the coagulation.

For me, wandering and coagulation were the warp and weft of the form that was emerging. I wandered back to Brazil for a time and retrieved parts of myself and left parts of myself there. I wandered through hospital hallways as a nurse and fumbled with espresso machines as a barista. I wandered my way through sagging open mics and empty midnight shows. I wandered the pages of books that would seed my formless mind with new visions. I wandered around ideas that would fall into my formless days, making paths where there had been no path. I wandered the landscapes of the emotions that would visit and meet my heart. I wandered my way into depth psychology and archetypes and myth. The wandering slowly stitched my life back together. My life slowly took form again—nothing fancy, but definitely handmade.

Wandering has a profoundly important place in the life of the deep psyche and soul, and yet so often in our culture it is taboo to wander. This is not coincidental. For the homogenous systems to keep grinding out our lives and our reality, we each have to stay on track. We have to stay productive. We have to justify our reasons for actions and desires within the context of functionality, productivity, and arrival. We have already been told what we should hope for and our task is to effort relentlessly toward that goal.

But what of the times when you don't know where you want to go? What of the times when all you know is not this anymore? What of when our knowing lives thrust us out of the illuminated ring of light into shadowy and unknown terrain? Yes, as Dr. Clarissa Pinko-la Estés says, at these thresholds "to wander is a very good choice."[58]

Wandering is not only a profound necessity to the life of the wild soul but is also a revolutionary act of transgression toward a consciousness that demands goal, outcome, and product.

Wandering as resistance.

Wandering as spiritual practice.

Wandering as prayer.

Wandering as play and rest.

Wandering as a way of knowing.

Sometimes, like Eve, we are simply walking through our days when we stumble upon something that causes our whole lives to change. We don't plan for it. In the liminal space of wandering we hear the whisper of truth stopping us in our tracks. In the wandering we are attuned to the signs and omens that populate our pathless path. We follow our intuition, and we take the time to listen and look. Wandering makes space for the powerful magic of curiosity.

# CURIOSITY

*When it's over, I want to say: all my life*
*I was a bride married to amazement.*
*I was the bridegroom, taking the world into my arms.*
*I don't want to end up simply having visited this world.*

**Mary Oliver**[59]

As Eve walked, she heard something—a voice both secretive and strong. The serpent, ancient guardian of the sacred tree, spoke and told Eve that she would not die if she ate the fruit of knowledge. The serpent assured her that if she ate the fruit she would become like God, knowing good and evil. The consummate good girl, Eve added restrictions of her own, since the commandment was to not eat the fruit, Eve decided she wouldn't even touch it. Eve remained in her obedience. But the serpent persisted. And Eve paused. Interrupted, she stopped. Her obedient mind said no, but curiosity turned her toward what was forbidden. Curiosity drew her into the creative transgression toward sovereignty. If Eve had remained in a posture of judgment rather than curiosity, the moment would have been missed. If she had remained in unquestioned obedience severed from lived experience, she would not have noticed the stirrings of her body and the beauty of the fruit. She was curious enough to listen, and then to look and see. And then to reach and taste.

About ten years after that Tuesday on the lawn chair, I wandered into a used bookstore in Seattle. It was a time when the *coagulatio* was beginning, my inner life was taking shape again after years of formlessness and wandering. Shortly after this day my dear friend and I would start our year of study and inquiry into the feminine sacred. During this particular wander, I stumbled upon a book that made me stop and look. It was called *Women Who Run with the Wolves: Myths and Stories of the Wild Woman Archetype* by Clarissa Pinkola Estés. I knew nothing about it, but it caught my attention, and sparked my curiosity. I bought it for seven dollars and took it home.

Winter was already descending with its long darkness and gray skies. I needed some good books to read in front of my little space heater between shifts at the pediatric psychiatric unit at the local children's hospital where I worked as a nurse. For weeks, I fell headlong into the book and its myths and images: wise and ruthless grandmothers, too-good mothers, lost orphans, cruel predators, visible and invisible helpers. Each chapter was uncovering ancient wisdom that lived in the stories, but also in my own body and ancestral memory. Over and within all of it was the Bone Gatherer, the one who sings over the bones and brings life back to what we thought was lost forever.

Reading that book was a homecoming. After so long wandering and grieving, this book sparked something in me. It awakened me to the truth that I could live symbolically again; I could sing over the bones in my own life. I could live soulfully and meaningfully without having to go back to the way I did that before. I could still be a mystic. As I read through each myth and chapter, I was in awe at the way the author guided me into the realm of the deep and wild psyche. She stitched story and life together through a powerful metaphoric sensibility. It changed my life. And I was so curious about what she was doing and how.

Around the same time, I read another book that had a significant impact on my life. It was *The Care of the Soul: A Guide for Cultivating Depth and Sacredness in Everyday Life* by Thomas Moore. The ideas were new to me and yet I deeply recognized them. It was like I was learning a language that enabled me to speak of my experiences. It was a language I was just learning but somehow had also always known. These two books offered me images, stories, ideas, and language that I acutely needed as I lived into new ways of being in the world, and I was very curious. I followed the curiosity and discovered that they were depth psychologists. I followed my curiosity further, for years, and eventually found myself in a graduate program getting a PhD in depth psychology. I am endlessly grateful to my curiosity for so faithfully guiding me closer to home.

In patriarchal consciousness we are taught early on what is considered good/favorable/acceptable and what is not. It is a hierarchal way of being, after all, and so relies fundamentally on binaries and distinctions like these. This can be so ingrained in the way we experience the world, that we may immediately and unconsciously make a judgment about something we encounter. Without even realizing it, we place it the 'good' or 'bad' category without looking at it more closely or even paying attention to what just showed up.

For example, you may have grown up in a community that considered anger unacceptable. Later, when feelings of anger come up you may not actually pay attention and tend to those feelings and their contexts as you automatically label them 'bad' and work to fix, disappear, or ignore this unacceptable visitor. Or if envy shows up you may immediately turn on yourself with stories of shame about how you are petty or should be grateful and how you need to find a way to fix that as soon as possible.

Learning to choose curiosity over judgment is an incredibly transgressive act. It is a subversive practice and is a powerful aid in dismantling internalized hierarchy and disrupting external systems of exclusion. The power of a pause just before the moment of judgment opens up space for curiosity. Curiosity is a friendly and gentle engagement with the unknown; it opens portals into new possibilities.

The Wild Pause is a practice that can help us cultivate a curious posture. It is the breath space that allows us to consciously choose curiosity over judgment. It is the practice of greeting each experience as it arrives. That is, when an emotion, thought, or attitude is noticed, rather than immediately determining what it is based on a predetermined formula—i.e., envy is bad, therefore, something is wrong with me or something is wrong with the other—we take a moment to look and see who or what is visiting. We pay attention. With the envy, for example, we notice it and take that breath, that pause. *Okay there is envy knocking at my door unbidden again. I don't like it. I wish it would go away. But I wonder what message it is bringing, why is it here?* In the space of the pause we are free to choose curiosity.

When you do this, you may discover a variety of things. You may discover that your soul is speaking of a deep longing that is going untended. You may discover that you are having a difficult time accepting and loving your own fate. You may discover that you are continually living in an attitude of scarcity. Had you simply judged the arrival of envy as bad or regressive and slammed the door in its face, you may have missed the opportunity to listen. Most importantly, you would have missed the opportunity to see and know and love your life more deeply.

What if our first and most important task is to take care of, nurture, befriend, and love the life we have been given? I like to imagine my life as a tender and wild creature that I hold close, watching and learning its ways and creating an environment where it will feel safe, free, loved, and true. This loving stewardship is one of the ways we cultivate inner friendship and belonging. The Wild Pause helps us develop a sensibility of welcome and spaciousness as we get to know these tender wild creatures and learn to love them.

Imagine being entrusted with the care of a child but continually shunning their experience if you didn't agree with it, weren't comfortable with it, didn't understand it, didn't like it, or didn't have time for it. So that each time the child brought you one of these experiences you simply ignored it, hurried to label and fix it, or actively tried to make it disappear. We can imagine that this child may not feel loved. We can imagine that this child would have great difficulty thriving under such harsh and cruel environments. And yet, this is often what we do to our own tender wild lives. Learning to welcome our lives with curiosity is a powerful way to be with and to see our lives in new ways.

Curiosity and attention walk hand in hand. Curiosity *requires* attention. And often, close attention requires slowness. Archetypal psychologist James Hillman wrote about the practice of *notitia*, "a primary activity of the soul…that capacity to form true notions of things from attentive noticing."[60] He linked lack of noticing with insatiable need for consumption, claiming that "to notice each event would limit our appetite for events."[61] Curiosity and close attention slow us down. They feed the soul and nourish the imagination. Curiosity invites us into another radical perspective: multiplicity.

From an archetypal perspective we are naturally polytheistic, always inviting the manifold ways of being and knowing. From this posture, we are continually asking at each juncture who is visiting, who must be invoked and honored at this particular threshold. Sometimes Ariadne is required. Sometimes Psyche. Sometimes Eve. From an archetypal perspective there are many sacred ways of being and knowing, so, we relinquish the tyranny of trying to find the One Way and ask instead, *Which way is called for right now?* When we live this way, we do not serve one way of being but many. This is the work of discernment through worship and devotion to our largeness—a "ceaseless baptism of *this too belongs.*"[62]

Archetypal reality is multiplicitous and our work and play of re-enchantment is to learn to see more and more, to let more in, to perceive the mythic and archetypal realities running through our lives, and then to participate meaningfully with the life all around us and within us. To do this we must cultivate a true curiosity and attention. When we pause and suspend judgment (conscious or unconscious), we open up space for more possibilities to emerge. So, at times, Ariadne's calculated, patient, and cunning way is the archetypal altar we find ourselves at, and once we recognize, or see through the everyday into the mythic realities of our lives, we participate in her way of being. We plan, consult, research, and wait for the right moment. At other times, like Eve, we wander, and in the wandering find our knowing.

Sometimes transgressions from old stable forms into new ones are birthed out of experiences of sheer otherness and overt oppression. In other words, the transgression is motivated by rejection of the old oppressive ways. It is an active leaving, and maybe even destroying, of something. Sometimes it is hearing a whisper of knowing and feeling the humming of the body as we follow our desire and reach for something beautiful. The word *sometimes* is a powerful antidote, a subtle but strong medicine, that challenges the hierarchy and singularity many of us have been trained in. It is a simple but powerful spell. It quietly transgresses the idea of The One and invites us into a posture of curiosity, multiplicity, and continual discernment.

Sometimes, like Eve, you may be simply walking through your days when you stumble upon something that causes your whole life to change. You don't plan for it, but in the liminal space of wandering you may hear the whisper of truth stopping you in your tracks. You may pause and get curious. You may pay attention and listen to the signs and omens along the way. Like Eve, you may take the time to listen and look. And when you see and desire, you may reach and feed yourself.

Eve's way is a way of the senses; it is the way of pleasure. Eve sees that the fruit is beautiful. In her wandering and in her curiosity, she understands that the fruit is good for beauty, pleasure, nourishment, and knowing…and she reaches for the fruit. She brings the ripe fruit to her lips, takes a bite of it, and makes the fruit a part of her body: the flesh and the fruit become one.

# PLEASURE & THE WAY
# OF THE SENSES

*Pleasure is not one of the spoils of capitalism. It is what
our bodies, our human systems, are structured for; it is
the aliveness and awakening, the gratitude and humility,
the joy and celebration of being miraculous.*

**adrienne maree brown**[63]

I often sit with folks who are filled with unrest, with an unnamed longing. As they walk through the duties of daily life, a song hums just below the surface—sometimes hauntingly beautiful, sometimes deeply disruptive like fingernails on a chalkboard. This song, they know on some level, is the song calling them back to themselves, back to a cadence that makes sense to their wild creature self. As we invite and explore what is showing up with curiosity rather than judgment, we often find a deep sadness and overwhelming exhaustion. There is a sense that everything is being given away or taken. That time is a relentless ticking. That the tasks of living and loving are siphoning the life force from them. That everything is accomplished through titanic effort of will rather than through natural response.

As we explore this, I often see something interesting happen when we get to the point of recognition that the wild self is wilting under the pressures of an obedient and too crowded life. I see the grief of what has been lost and the relief of naming the longing. And then I see the solutions, usually in the form of resolutions and lists, begin to populate the space. *Okay*, they say, *I need to do less of that and more of this. I need to learn to say no. I need to take more baths. I need to stop trying to please everyone...* As this unfolds, I witness the heaviness of exhaustion return, often increased.

So quickly the call of the soul for more ease and more freedom and more wildness becomes a litany of more duties to accomplish. Which requires more efficiency, more will, and more productivity. Often what is happening is that once we notice that the deep self is calling for more attention, we bring up the map we were handed and begin the work of reaching that ideal. Currently many often call this 'self-care.' It is wise to ask ourselves: *Is this another ideal image of what I should be and do? Is this ideal inviting me into another form of the obedient life?* The shadow of our overthrow is that we may inadvertently simply replace our punishing gods and demanding ideals. The shadows of wellness and therapeutic culture, for example, are teeming with punishing gods and prescribed ideals. Again, developing the ability to see into the shadows, although difficult at times, offers the opportunity to find more of our nature and more freedom. It is useful to pay attention to feelings of striving, exhaustion, or resignation when you make these lists. Even the fantasy of self-care can be a punishing god.

I have wondered much about this. What can support us in finding more ease and freedom in our own natures without adding lists, solutions, and ultimately shame and guilt to our days? Often it is the right question that makes doors where previously we only knew stone walls. The right question serves as a soft lantern, gently guiding our next steps toward home. In this case, I have found the question, *Where is my pleasure?* to be a powerful lantern.

This question, with its soft light, guides us away from the litany of obedience to an external mandate and brings us directly into our bodies and into presence. It has the power to slowly or suddenly break the blind hold of our indoctrination to continually strive toward a faraway ideal and bring us to the exact moment we are inhabiting. It brings us into the immediacy of sensation. Pleasure in all of its forms—emotional, physical, spiritual, psychological—brings us into the immediacy of sensation experienced through the body in this present moment, not as a punishing god declaring his commandments from the heavens, but as whisper, fire, tingle, arousal, or inspiration. It causes us to consult with our senses and to move through in a sensual way. *What can I hear, touch, see, and smell? Where is the stirring of beauty filling my body with wonder and desire? Where is the nourishing energy flowing? Where do I feel the spark of inspiration or vision?* These questions can be powerful and loving guides as we transgress the paradigms that have taught us to know without the wisdom of body, pleasure, and beauty.

In many religious and secular paradigms, we are asked and even forced to know without consulting body, desire, and pleasure. For example, in a capitalistic paradigm we are indoctrinated to know what to do and who to be through approximation to the capitalistic ideal, and so we measure our lives by how much wealth we accumulate, how high we can get in the hierarchy of power, how religiously we participate in the fantasy of growth without reflection. We are often coerced into making decisions almost entirely based on productivity and efficiency. What makes sense is what fits into these values and to desire for anything outside of these values is considered foolish and even dangerous. In this scenario, not only are body, desire, and pleasure not acknowledged as valid sources of knowing, they are often confronted as obstacles to be conquered on the way to success.

Even our everyday instincts are under continual attack. I often feel bombarded by the latest ideal of how I should eat, stay hydrated, sleep, and move. And this is further problematized by the fact that so many of us, as a result of this, have injured instincts in these basic areas of our animal existence. Thankfully, recently there have been more voices encouraging us to do something profoundly radical: to pay attention and listen to how things feel in our bodies. This return to the senses is a powerful way of knowing. But still, knowing through the stirrings of the body, the longing for beauty, and the call of pleasure is often devalued and demonized. And to follow them is transgressive, and again, Eve has something to teach us about this.

Eve knows through her senses; her way is a sensual way. Eve's transgression was not ideological or theoretical. Her transgression involved reaching hands, the sensuality of taste buds, and inglorious digestive juices. It is embodied action. Eve does not seem to be compelled by ideals and abstractions but by the nearness of physical experience and felt intuition. Eve's way of transgressing is created with each unplanned, intuitive step until she takes in the fruit. Eve wanders into her transgression, guided by instinct and body. Sometimes transgressions rely on clarity of thought and careful use of resources as the guiding lights, like Ariadne's. Eve uses her senses as her guiding lights.

She walks.

She listens.

She sees.

She touches.

She tastes.

Eve knows through her body. This is the miracle: she trusts her senses more than the story she was told. She trusts her hunger more than the warning. She trusts what she sees more than the instructions she was handed. She trusts her own authority. And so, too, may it be for us.

# A NOTE ON BODY

*You only have to let the soft animal of your body*
*Love what it loves...*

**Mary Oliver**[64]

The body is a central part of Eve's mythic transgression, carrying and guiding her into sovereignty. Ironically, the traditional interpretation of the myth has also centred the body, but in that interpretation, it has been cast as the fulcrum of evil. In the traditional interpretation, Eve's transgression is said to have brought sin and death into the world in and through the body.

Augustine famously used the Eden story as the foundation of his doctrine of original sin, "The sin which they [the first parents] committed was so great that it impaired all human nature—in this sense, that the nature has been transmitted to posterity with a propensity to sin and a necessity to die."[65] In this theory, Adam and Eve did not only lose their own state of harmony, they caused death and depravity to enter the whole human race, a state of sin that is passed on through sex. In this doctrine, not only are body and sex evil, every human body born is contaminated with the sin of Eve and Adam. At the center of all this evil is the body—the body in sex, the body giving birth, and the body being birthed are all imagined as inherently evil because of Eve's transgression.

Of course, this idea of the body as evil has moved far beyond the walls of the church. The desacrilization of the body lives in ideas of body as machine, body as product, body as commodity, body as object. In the quest for human ascension, patriarchal consciousness, in many ways, has sought to leave the body behind.

In the Great Reversal—the mythological movement that the Eden story is a part of—a shift was happening between matriarchal and patriarchal consciousness as the Sky Fathers defeated and banished the Earth Mothers. This shift affected not only how we view creator/creatress but also how we view what was created. In the older mythic images, born from the body of the great mothers, creation remained a part of its creatress. Creatress and creation were made of the same substance. When Sky Fathers began to speak creation into being, creation was no longer imagined as the offspring of the sacred.

Specifically, in Genesis we find a cosmos created from the word of Yahweh. Here, we are not born from body and do not share flesh. Not only is the body left out of the birthing process, this image also shows that flesh—body and Earth—are separate and distinct from spirit (i.e., Yahweh's disembodied word). In this move, humans and Earth became products that were deemed "good" and neither was part of "God's body."[66] In this imagination we are no longer the offspring of gods and goddesses. We are the technology, the product, of the gods.

Of course, there are many factors that shape our cultures and societies. And again, our creation myths are deeply significant factors in this unfolding and have a symbiotic relationship with how we live.

*What happens when we begin to imagine that our mother and the intimacy of her body were banished, and that we were made by the word of a distant body-less spirit? What happens when we imagine that rather than connecting us to the sacred, our bodies serve as a symbol of difference and separation? What happens when we imagine that body and Earth are filled with evil and that only trust in a male sky spirit will save us?* As I reflect on these questions and on how we have treated and imagined our bodies and the Earth in Sky Father cultures, it becomes apparent, once again, how our myths become how we live.

I find that my relationship with flesh—body and Earth—is an

ever-unfolding tale. It has been a difficult unfolding. Incarnation, to become flesh, can be painful. Slowly and unevenly, I continue to learn to be more here—enfleshed and in flesh.

I love this flesh.

I fear this flesh.

The veil between flesh and no flesh is so thin. This soft animal is magnificent and also so fierce, ready to destroy. Ready to change everything. Ready to swallow whole. The vulnerability of bodies terrifies me. Before I go to bed at night, I check on my sleeping son. I stand over him in the quiet of the night, watching and listening for every breath as though the world depended on that ritual. As though the act of concentrated attention would keep us all safe. I watch his small and growing body moving rhythmically to his breath and I wish I was filled with joy and with gratitude—I try to tell myself that is what is happening—but my body tells me the deeper truth through tense muscles, pounding heart, held breath: I am filled with terror. I fear the loss of body. Bodies remind me of what will be lost. And yet, it is this reality that has most powerfully taught me to love my body and to seek to inhabit it more and more, even if that process is messy and difficult sometimes.

There is only one thing that seems to be beyond question about the moment of our death: we will no longer be in these bodies. *Someday I will no longer be in this particular body.* My heart is filled with a deep ache when I let this truth sit with me. My heart swells with love. I feel the full force of my love for this body—this tender animal that knows and remembers every moment of my life. And that, without a doubt, we will be separated someday.

This soft animal, this body, reminds me of who I have been, who I am, and of who I am becoming. This body knows more, sees all, remembers everything. This flesh carries everything I refuse to hold and all the secrets I keep even from myself. This flesh is connected and made of the Great Mother; I am substance of her substance. This body is home and reminds me every day that I am Nature. The pulsing blood, hard bone, rubbery muscle, shedding skin, the dance of continual filling and emptying of the heart and of lungs inflating and deflating, reminds me every day that Nature is not a machine. I love my body.

I have found this love of my body is distinct from how I feel about what I look like, I think of body image and love of body as different conversations. I have found that I can have a moment when I truly dislike how my body looks, and also in that same moment be deeply in love with this body. Sometimes, our collective conversation about freeing the body from harmful constructs and ideologies can become reduced to grappling with issues of body image. Untangling our relationship with our body image is so important and is transgressive of a narrative that imagines our bodies as commodities and uses our bodies as pawns in the violence of hierarchy and power-over. And it is also important to notice that we can be involved in transgressive conversations about body image without ever moving beyond the story of body as object. Love of body invites us to move beyond body as object into body as sacred animal; body as close companion; body as deep witness; body as friend; body as beloved.

May we remember and choose love next time we hear our bodies discussed as objects, as products, as machines. Let us call forth tenderness as antidote to this cruelty. We are flesh. We are a liminal incarnation. Why offer anything but love and nurture to these soft animals? Oh, it is difficult when we are in a way of being that includes our bodies so intricately in its systems of hierarchy and power-over. May our revolt be awareness, social action, and political change. And also, may our resistance arrive in the form of fierce and tender love, today, for our own bodies.

# LONGING & DESIRE

*Longing is the impulse of the soul calling us deeper into life. It says, 'It's time to go home.' It is a piercing ache in the heart that knows there is more than this and pulls us, like a magnet, in orientation towards it.*

**Toko-pa Turner**[67]

In Portuguese we have a beautiful word: *saudade*. It means to miss, to ache for, to long for. You don't have it, you are with *saudade* like a close companion. *Saudade* is a way of being. The closest word we have for it in English is longing.

I recently talked with a woman who was in the midst of a transgressive move out of constricting patterns and into more spacious places. Like the vine wrapped around that tree, old stories were tightening around her, trying to convince her that she would never be free. They told her she would never grow and spill over the too-small boundaries she had been living. Tears came as she expressed her fear that she would not be able to choose a different way, that she wouldn't know how to live differently. What I saw, as I sat witnessing and accompanying her, was a woman filled with profound and fierce longing for her own life. And I wasn't worried at all. "I trust your longing," I told her. I was filled with a faith that her fierce and tender longing would not leave her. The *Great Saudade* would lead her home.

Many have claimed that Eve reached for the fruit because she was weak, gullible, stupid, malicious, and proud. But the myth shows us something different. The myth shows us that Eve reached for the fruit because she saw something beautiful, and she wanted what it offered. When Eve saw that the fruit was beautiful, good for nourishment, and good for knowing, she desired it and her longing became louder than her obedience. In that moment of awakened desire and felt longing, Eve reached for the fruit and chose to follow her own instincts over external mandate. Perhaps we could say that Eve desired the fruit because it showed itself as a way toward what she longed for: beauty, pleasure, nourishment, and knowing.

Longing is a powerful way of knowing. A lighthouse on the horizon, our deepest longings protect us from getting lost. Our truest longings can be openings in our being that connect us to everything else, like a spiritual umbilical cord. It may feel like an ache-filled emptiness, but it is not empty, it is open.[68] And this kind of longing keeps us in communion with the mysteries. I imagine it as the hollow thread at the core of our being. Longing has the power to keep us alive and nourished, and it continually beckons us into more closeness with the lives we have been given.

Longing and desire are interconnected, and they also live different lives. While longing is the lighthouse on the horizon, desire is the lantern that illuminates the next step. Desire, with its immediate want, can often be satisfied. But there is something about longing, that deep ache, the *Great Saudade*, that can only be tended to, followed, worshipped, loved, held. Desire has a feeling of fire, of urgency; to desire is to be awakened. Desire brings with it a sense of immediacy, while longing evokes something distant and just beyond the horizon.

It has been a tragedy that so often in patriarchal consciousness our desire and our longing have been used against us—tragic but not surprising. Desire is an admission of agency. It is an admission of a self. Remember the *Malleus Maleficarum*? It named two of the greatest evils a person could demonstrate are lust and ambition. The presence of desire is the proof of the presence of a person, whole and alive. Desire is a threat to subjugation and objectification. Sexual desire is a threat to the idea of a being that is imagined only in relation to another. Spiritual desire is a threat to the idea of a being who is created to serve and be subservient to the unquestioned authority of an-other. *Desire is a direct threat to obedience.* Desire is proof of personhood. We can see in the example of the *Malleus Maleficarum*, that a woman's desire has been used as justification for violence, exile, and murder. Not coincidentally, in this paradigm desire was the proof of her evil.

Longing, the portal within and the lighthouse on the horizon, is also a threat to the obedient life. Longing is simultaneously a pull into our own depths, where we move toward our belonging in the life of all things, and a pull toward the unknown horizon. Deep longing for our truest home and wildest life creates space for our largeness and calls that expansiveness into reality. Both the descent into our own depths and our reach for the horizon are transgressive in a paradigm that demands obedience, stability, and surface living. Longing threatens the status quo when it becomes stronger than obedience.

Longing and desire call us to deepen our imagination and to envision other possible worlds. They open our eyes and allow us to see past the illusions of a too-small world into the potentialities of living more expansive and truer lives. They help us ask this tiny but mighty question: *Is there another way?* Through longing and desire, we might find the strength and vision we need to transgress the life of obedience as we move closer to our wild belonging. Like siren songs, they call us into imagination, body, and Nature as ways of knowing.

For centuries the Eden story has been used as weapon against our longing and our desire. The warning has been clear: *Do not trust your own body, desire, or longing. Do not trust what you see and feel*

*and hear. Only trust external authority. Only trust what you have been told by those with power.* This message has not only been repeated in various ways, it has been regularly reinforced. The punishment is often swift and violent for those who step beyond the bounds of obedience. And indeed, the moment of desire and longing was the pivotal moment that turned Eve toward the transgression. She considered the words of the serpent and she remembered the words of Yahweh. She stopped. She looked. What she saw was beauty, nourishment, and wisdom. I imagine that in that moment she desired the fruit and longed for beauty, nourishment, and knowing because when she saw them, she reached, and she ate the fruit. However, instead of the death she had been promised, her eyes were opened and she became like the gods. In other words, desire and longing led her to knowing and sovereignty.

Eve's desire was the beautiful fruit. Her longing for what the sacred tree offered pulled the transgression forward. In a story that has been used as weapon against Nature, we find the wisdom of the more-than-human world shining at its center.

# MORE-THAN-HUMAN NATURE

*On one side of the world were people whose relationship with the living world was shaped by Skywoman, who created a garden for the well-being of all. On the other side was another woman with a garden and a tree. But for tasting its fruit, she was banished from the garden and the gates clanged shut behind her.*

**Robin Wall Kimmerer**[69]

One morning a few years after moving out of the city, I wrote this after my habitual morning walk to let the goats out of their enclosure:

*My early walk on the land this morning is a wordless prayer. I wave goodbye to my son and walk to the Cedar. I listen to the water of the small cascade and meandering stream, a subtle medicine. I lean my body onto the body of the Cedar. I do this most mornings and evenings. This morning, as my body leans on her trunk with my heart as close to her as possible, I feel home. I immediately feel the calm of her history and deep rootedness.*

*Whatever energy is swirling in my body slows down and feels held. I breathe with her. After a while, I walk down to the Grandmother's spot—a little ledge nestled beside a pine tree west of the unruly garden. It overlooks the ravine where the waters run through, again I can hear water falling among the cedars, alderwoods, pines, and maples. I stand in a circle of trees and I wonder if by the time I die I will have become as much a part of this land as these trees—my body and presence belonging as much in the life of this land as the waters, birds, rabbits, cougars, owls, snakes, and ravens. I stand still and internally offer a deep bow of silent reverence as my supplication: may this be so.*

*I take a deep breath.*

*Spring is arriving, somehow both gently and fiercely. Gentle in its softness as tender new life emerges from the dark soil and from closed buds and from hidden nests. Fierce in its relentless, though quiet, arrival. Hundreds of berry bushes are waking up—salmonberries first, then huckleberries and thimbleberries and finally, by August, the blackberries will complete their aggressive arrival. The bees are doing their work. The chickadees sing to each other every morning, and since I hear only their calls of play and communication and not their calls of distress, I am reassured that all is well in the forest. The ferns are uncurling themselves like tiny fists and soon will cover most of the land. The yellow buds of the maple trees are small honeycombs in the slanted morning light. The tender pink flowers of the salmonberry bushes promise pleasure and abundance humming just beyond reach. I hear a rustling in the bushes that I cannot identify, and I remind the creatures I am here in peace. I am overwhelmed with love and gratitude for this land, who holds me and shows me what I am made of.*

This is the glorious truth: we are Nature. We came from Her and will return to Her. We are made of stardust. Our bones are made from the minerals of the Earth. Our blood and cells are filled with Her waters. The neuronal pathways in our brains mirror the patterns of the galaxies moving toward each other.

We are Nature.

And yet, we have lived in a style of consciousness that imagines humans as separate—and above—the rest of Nature. This violent severing has had devastating impact. Even here, we must not speak of the impact on Earth and then the impact upon humans, as though we were not one magnificent living breathing organism—as though we were not One Flesh.[70] Our Body is continually used as resource,

carved and chiseled in violent acts of commodification and objectification. Our Waters polluted, diverted, stolen, and vanishing. Our
expressions of our ourselves in all of our multiplicity becoming ex-
tinct with each passing moment.

This severance is a forgetting of what we are. It is loss of belonging.
It is dis-enchantment.

Mythologist Joseph Campbell made correlations between the
Eden story and the Western paradigm's relationship with Nature,
linking this dis-enchantment to the fall from Eden. He attributed,
in a mythic sense, the birth of a desacralized and lifeless cosmos in
the Western imagination to the fall from Eden, i.e., the moment of
Eve's transgression and subsequent expulsion from the Garden. This
is part of the curse in the Garden: paradisaical harmony and union
are over, instead, we are cursed to live in separation from and in constant struggle with the land.

The Eden story was a part of the much larger mythological and
archetypal movement of the Great Reversal, displacing the Earth
Mother Goddess in favor of the Sky Father God. Since the Earth
itself was born from the body of the Great Mother, the move of eradicating her life-generating womb and bestowing her powers of fertility
upon the word of the Father God was also a move involved in erasing
our understanding of the essence of Nature as divine.[71] As creation
lost the status of offspring and moved to category of good product,
Nature began to lose its sacredness in the mythic imagination.

The sense of the interconnection and interrelatedness of all
things—since creation was the offspring of the divine and part of
her substance—was replaced by a sense of separation and duality.
Nature as flesh and as substance of the divine became the product
and technology of the gods. Creator and creation, heaven and earth,
male and female, night and day, light and dark, these were all separated and made distinct, and were organized hierarchically, in this
new imagination.

When I finished the coursework for my doctoral degree, I took a quarter off before beginning to research and write my dissertation. My family and I decided to rent out our small Seattle house for a few months to go live on a small island in the Puget Sound—a thirty-minute ferry ride from the city. We found a tiny blue cabin on a hill overlooking the sea and the city across the channel. I was teaching at a local college at the time, so would go into the city once or twice a week for long classes and would spend the rest of my time on the island with my four-year old son. It was magical. There was only one place we could walk to from our little home, a café with outdoor seating and picnic table under an old oak tree. We walked there often for treats and something to do.

One day on the walk back to our cabin, someone told us that there were orcas swimming by the bluff. We ran toward the overlook and as we ran, eagles flew overhead. I felt a deep sense of wonder and participation. When we arrived at the edge of the bluff, others were already gathered there in hopeful expectation. The sun was out, and it was a beautiful day. After only a few moments, we saw them. The orcas swimming, jumping, playing. We were mesmerized. My son and I stood on that bluff and watched until the orcas were out of sight, disappearing into the horizon and into the depths.

Weeks later on another increasingly rare sunny day as autumn descended upon the Puget Sound, I took a walk along the same bluff and looked at those deep waters where the orcas had passed through. Again, I was filled with wonder. As I looked over the ocean and imagined all the life hidden in her dark underwater womb, I wondered about this idea that the Earth is becoming conscious. As I ruminated, I suddenly began to laugh out loud at the absurdity of the situation: here I was, a part of the Earth and made of her substance, wondering and pondering the possibility of Earth developing the ability to wonder and ponder.

The act of wondering about the consciousness of Earth is an acknowledgement of a deep and foundational belief of Western modernity: that humans are not Nature. By not recognizing our wonderings as somehow Her wonderings, we unconsciously confess our exile from our belonging. Jung wrote that the tragedy of modernity is our "loss of roots."[72] We have been severed from our deep instinctual lives and it has made us profoundly ill.

In the literalized and traditional interpretation of the Eden story, not only is the One Flesh cursed—the Earth and the Body—they actually caused the Fall to begin with. Eve walked in the Garden, admiring the trees. She listened to the animal—a serpent—and saw that the fruit offered her pleasure, knowledge, and nourishment. She saw the attractive qualities of the fruit, "When the woman saw that the fruit of the tree was good for food and pleasing to the eye, and also desirable for gaining wisdom, she took some and ate it."[73] Her senses led her, and she reached, and she tasted the fruit.

If this transgression is interpreted as the cause of the great, immutable fall of Nature from grace and belonging into death and depravity, then Earth, body, and the animal voice are not to be trusted. This distrust is, of course, further reinforced by the proclamation of a cursed female body destined for pain and subjugation, and a cursed male body at war with the land. The curse that Yahweh pronounced after the transgression stated, "Cursed is the ground because of you; through painful toil you will eat of it."[74] In this vision, Nature itself is the cause of the fall and is also the bearer of the punishment for the fall.

It is a profound tragedy that this story, surrounded by impoverished imagination, has led to the denigration of Nature. In its literalized form, this image has implicated the Earth and Body with evil and cast them into the shadows. However, as we return the Eden story to its mythic home, loosening it from the grip of the literal and traditional interpretation, we find again that what has been called evil is actually one of the powerful liberating elements of the story. The myth shows us that the trust and communion with the natural world at the heart of the transgression led to sovereignty, not depravation or certain death. The wisdom and sacredness of the more-than-human world—serpent, sacred tree, fruit—offer Eve what she needs and move her on in creative transgression toward new consciousness.

Eve shows a way of knowing through leaning into the wisdom of more-than-human nature—a term coined by David Abram that refers to the part of Nature that is not human, loosening us from the harmful binary of human and Nature as two separate realities.[75] On a mythological level, we understand Eve taking in the fruit from the sacred tree guarded by a serpent as an ancient symbol for communing with the Goddess. That is, she is in communion with and in devotion to the ways of being and knowing linked to images of the feminine sacred, that up until then had been complimentary images to the wholeness of the symbolism of the divine and human experiences of the mysteries we inhabit. Eve shows trust in the wisdom of instinct and more-than-human nature. She listens to the counsel of the serpent and she makes the fruit of the tree a part of her body. Even as on one level Eve is being exiled because of eating the fruit from the tree, she also finds sovereignty and knowing through the fruit and through Asherah—the Branch Goddess, the Tree of Life, the Serpent Lady. Eve is exiled from the Garden in a moment of deep embodied communion with Asherah and with more-than-human nature. It is both a moment of exile and of liberation, severance and communion.

This is a poignant image for us today. As we seek to address the ecological crisis and our human relationship with the Earth, Eve reminds us of ways that have been buried in a dominant paradigm that has favored mastery over participation. The hubristic fantasy of human dominion is challenged by a posture of interdependence and love. As the more-than-human world compels Eve into new consciousness and as its wisdom inhabits a central position in the story, the view of creation as a distinct product of the Sky Father is put into dialogue with the view of creation as sacred flesh and offspring of the Earth Goddess. The wisdom and sacredness of the more-than-human world is lifted out of the shadows and illuminated in consciousness. We are invited into communion.

The traditional interpretation of the Eden story has been used mercilessly by an age that has emphasized reason, transcendence, and spirit-less matter. We have become untethered from the body, from the soil, and from place. And as Jung stated, "Life that is not lived here, or the life lived provisionally, is utterly unsatisfactory."[76] A life that does not know its home—its textures, smells, moods, and its many faces—is a life without roots, a life without depths. It is an isolated and abstracted life.

As we scrub our surfaces clean, as we separate and sterilize our lives, Nature shows up in psycho-spiritual symptom. In other words, many of us have lost our sense of enchantment and suffer for it. This disenchantment severs us from ourselves and from our home. It causes us to lose the ability to see and experience a living and dynamic world, teeming with drama, creativity, and spirit.

May we reclaim a vision of a humanity that knows in its bones, in its soft rolling flesh, and it its warm pulsating bloodlines that it belongs to a much greater ecological system that includes the more-than-human world, that is part of One Flesh, that belongs to the world of animals, trees, soil, and rain.

May we reclaim what has been largely lost in Western modernity, that is, a human sense of deep connection, of mutual participation, and of unwavering belonging with and to Nature. In this vision, we return to what we are made of, or more accurately, we see what we are made of and feel it with our fingertips, catch its scent, taste its depths. We feel Nature's cadence beating in the depths of our bodies.

May we unravel the curse of disenchantment and return to wild belonging and old knowing. May we return to our roots and learn to participate in the great web of life of which we are a part of and enter consciously into the wild dance of the universe.

This is re-enchantment.

# BOOK FOUR:
# HOW SHALL WE THEN LIVE?

*Our ancestors will allow us to shout and shake at our gods, to
walk in the wilderness, to stare blankly upon our own being
and wonder: who am I to be? And when we learn the wisdom of
our ancestors and we drink in their love, we can turn away.*

*For they will be with us, cheering us on as we tread the
evolutionary path of all pioneers, visionaries, and simple surveyors.*

*We give away the known for that mysterious horizon.*

**Beverly Lanzetta**[77]

# THE MYTH OF SALVATION

*Dropping the salvational fantasy frees us up to the possibility of self-knowledge and self-acceptance, which are the very foundation of soul.*

**Thomas Moore**[78]

In Western paradigms we have been offered primarily one acceptable image for our lives: a life that moves forward, fast, and up on a linear path. We grow up. We move on. We climb the ladder. We overcome. We fall off track, and rush to get back on track. In other words, we are bound up in fantasies of ascension and transcendence.

Many of us have been indoctrinated within a salvational fantasy, whether that involves supplicating to a particular deity or simply drinking more water or accumulating more wealth. Humming just below the efficient and productive surfaces of our busy lives is the assumption that we are not good as we are right now, but if we only work hard enough, move fast enough, and get ahead and above enough, then we will reach that promised land—the place and time when we will finally be saved, where we will finally arrive and be called worthy. It is a terrible way to live. No wonder we are a culture exhausted and warring with ourselves and each other.

I wonder what the monotheisms would be like if they were not founded upon the need for salvation, without that foundational assumption that we need to be saved. I also wonder how successful consumerism would be without the salvational fantasy infusing our everyday lives. How well would products that promise improvement, transformation, and salvation—be it a car or a sweater—sell if they weren't predicated on our need to be better, healthier, sexier, holier, happier? I imagine not very well.

How would we live if we were not being haunted by the salvational fantasy?

In the hierarchical system of patriarchal consciousness, growth and forward movement are often unquestioned gods. In a blind rush to finally arrive at the place where we will be good enough, saved enough, rich enough, happy enough, or worthy enough, we take our cultural map and follow the yellow brick road that will take us to the elusive place called Salvation as fast as we can. The cycles of Nature are violently constricted as we silence our natural cadence of seasonal growth and decay, rise and descent, filling and emptying, in exchange for a linear path that will take us away as quickly and efficiently as possible from this fallen state and deliver us to our Arrival. In this frenzy, we often forget the expansiveness of our animality and adopt a method that is suited more for machine than animal.

And yet, when we hear our salvational fantasy and our obsession with ascension and improvement challenged, the internalized voices of our indoctrination might protest with warnings that we will slip into stagnation and entropy. In other words, there are many collective and personal admonishments that warn us to keep moving up, forward, and fast lest we fall into decay. Of course, in the realm of Nature decay is just as powerful of a deity as growth—one cannot exist without the other. But not only is this fear woven tightly into the collective worship of growth, it also may be tied in with a confusion that happens when we overlay hierarchical mechanistic thinking onto the ancient wisdom of Nature. Perhaps we have equated transformation with improvement, thinking them to be the same thing. And yet, they are not the same thing. And many systems of hierarchy and power-over have profited from this confusion and conflation.

Everything is always changing, revolving, adapting. Nature seems to have an inexorable dynamism and movement always at is center and periphery. But what if this constant transformation is about becoming, rather than improving? Is an acorn less worthy than an oak? Is an acorn just exactly and perfectly what it is, just as an oak is exactly and perfectly what it is? Yes. And yet they are in constant states of transformation. That is Nature. And we are Nature. Perhaps we have confused the powerful push of Life toward transformation as a punitive call for improvement rather than as an unwavering longing for our becoming, a deep and relentless faithfulness of our lives unto themselves.

I also wonder if we have confused a salvational fantasy with a healing fantasy. The salvational fantasy begins with an image of brokenness and assumes our natural state is one of depravity that we must overcome. In the salvational fantasy we cannot trust ourselves and must be saved from ourselves. On the other hand, the healing fantasy begins with an image of our wholeness and assumes our natural state is a desired way of being and works to return us to ourselves, to our nature. For me, this way of imagining opens up space for me to hold the need for personal and social change, while also holding the reality that we are not on an unyielding quest to leave our nature and finally arrive somewhere ahead and up where we will finally be okay. Transformation is understood as the constant becoming of Nature into more and more of itself, rather than an escape from Nature into salvation.

With the Eden story being used as a foundation for the propagation of a paradigm that relies on our depravity for its existence, this belief has taken root and flourished far beyond the walls of the Church. The legacy of the literalized Eve compels us to believe that Earth and Body cannot be trusted. Under the weight of this literalized interpretation of our origin story, all of us are bound—consciously and unconsciously—to live within a perpetual quest for spirit and for transcendence as we attempt to escape the evils of our own flesh, body, and Earth. We are forced to continually overcome the depravity of what it means to be sexual beings, a depravity and sexuality that are most poignantly carried in the curves of the female body and in the relentless generative powers of the Earth. We are propelled into insatiable need to regain the favor of the Father, while the Mother—along with her ways of knowing and her ways of being—is exiled with Eve.

The Eden story is tied to our collective idolization of ascension. With the starting point of being depraved and needing to be saved, we have become a society obsessed with transcendence and certainly our dominant religious institutions have offered the comfort and promise of this salvation, and have also profited from the fear of this damnation. If we are all bad and God is all spirit and above the earth and body, then it makes sense to continually seek to rise above this home, conveniently leaving Earth and body behind in a relentless search for salvation from our humanity.

*How would we live if we didn't need to be saved? How would we live if we were not caught in the grip of a salvational fantasy? What if we were born whole and good and had never unlearned how to live outside of the rhythms of our own nature?*

We have looked for our salvation in the heavens, in spirit, in transcendence. But if we shed the vision of our depraved bodies and cursed Earth, if we remember our wholeness and our belonging in Nature we might be lured by a fantasy of deepening, of growing down. If indeed we are born here to become more and more of what we are, to flourish and express Nature in the glory of her multiplicity, we might give up the singular fantasy of ascension and transcendence and allow ourselves to sink into the mud of the Earth. We might slow down enough to begin to feel the deeper rhythms of Nature calling us to grow down, further and further into her heart and into our deepest belonging.

This way of living would be a capitulation of the constant effort to rise above. It is an entering into the labor of presence and attention. It is a life devoted to immanence. It is a life devoted to small acts of presence, acts of worship to the joy of being here. It is a way of living that values growing up, but also knows the sacredness of growing down.

# THE ART OF GROWING DOWN

*Descent takes a while. We grow down, and we need a long life to get on our feet... To plant a foot firmly on earth – that is the ultimate achievement, and a far later stage of growth than anything begun in your head.*

**James Hillman**[79]

My father built our house, just as our community built every building on the land. We made our own red bricks with an old brick maker. Sometimes the children would sneak past the approved boundary back to where the men made the bricks and take turns getting in the manual cement mixer and spinning each other around in the rusty merry-go-round. Our house was always in progress, being added to and changed. I loved that house my dad built on the top of the hill. But my relationship with Home was always in flux. In the missionary world, one of the foundational tenets is that you are always ready to leave everything behind—your home, your job, your family, even in some ways your body—for God, for the good of the world. As a child I took this very seriously. It felt dangerous to desire anything but abandoned devotion to God. He was the only thing I couldn't lose. I felt this viscerally and probably daily.

I lived on a training base (that is what we called our community) for missionaries and people were continually arriving and then leaving to go to faraway places to serve God. I was continually heart broken by all the goodbyes. I learned to turn inward, to rely on nothing but what I called God. I made loss a practice. That is, I would imagine losing anything I loved in preparation and in the name of the only thing I could not lose: God. Of course, eventually I did lose that God, and my heart was shattered for many years.

I understood that I could not trust my body, my heart, or my desire since I was born fallen and in need of salvation (because of Eve). I could not love my house and the land I lived on too much in case God called me to leave it all behind (which he definitely would). I could not depend on my loved ones too much, because one day I would have to leave them, or they would leave me in the name of God. I practiced imagining myself making a beautiful life alone.

One of the ways I practiced loss was a "game" I played for years as I grew up. Any time I would pass through a depressed place, a desolate place filled with ugliness and suffering—whether in the slums of rural Brazil or in the outskirts of Katmandu or in crowded orphanages in Thailand—I would imagine myself living there. I would imagine myself making something beautiful out of the ugliness. I would imagine myself loving that place and those people. I would imagine a life in which I was okay—even there, even alone. I imagined many beautiful things made from scraps of ugliness and loneliness. I am grateful for what this practice cultivated in me. And, I can't help but notice the echoes of this practice reverberating in the underground room dream that told me my fate was to make something ugly, broken, and haunted into something beautiful. That was a very old story.

The only safe place to be was with God. The only safe thing to love was God. The only home I wouldn't lose was God. But all of this required me to learn to not really be here, on Earth, in my own life. It required that I not be in my fallen and dangerous body, not root into the cursed land where I lived, and not become entangled in my life in the world. Home was somewhere else. The true me was somewhere else far beyond the realms of toothbrushing and dishwashing, far beyond the pleasures of warm blankets, delicious food, and soft beds. True and lasting belonging were outside of the relationships populating my everyday life with love, pain, inspiration, sadness, and joy. In many ways, the call was to abandon myself and plant my life in an unseen disembodied spirit-soil with no mud, no shit, no nutrients, no matter. No being here.

In the salvational paradigm—whether in the context of religion, capitalism, or humanitarianism—our real lives are not here and now. Our real lives will be revealed when we finally shed these fallen bodies, leave this cursed Earth, and ascend into the place of spirit, free of matter and sin. Our real lives will begin when we finally arrive at enough health, wealth, success, or fame. Our lives will finally be worthy and right when we've done enough good work in the world.

What a strange and difficult way to imagine this miracle of temporary incarnation! It is no wonder we are obsessed with ascension—with growing up and moving forward. The last place we want to be is here. This is a story that lives in the fabric of our unconscious, whether we are aware of it or not, and for some of us more than others. These are some of the invisible forces we battle as we wrestle with what it means to be human, what it means to be a part of an ensouled world, what it means to be in rightful relationship with the more-than-human world and with our own bodies.

Transcendence is about rising above. Immanence is about indwelling, inhabiting. It is about growing down. It is about being here. It is about the numinosity of descent. It is about a life planted deeply in the soils of the muddy earth, watered and cultivated and pruned through lived experience. Immanence is about finding Home here and now, in these bodies and on this Earth.

Home is an elusive and numinous word. What does it mean to find home? There are many ways to describe or circle around this state, but most of all we have to feel into this mysterious internal place we call home. To be home is to feel safe and of one piece. It is to be in the grace of your elemental waters where your being is marked by presencing rather than efforting.[80] It is to fall into the rightness and rhythm of being who you are without shame. When we are home, we find our way through deep wild response rather than through unremitting willful effort.

To be too far from home for too long is to be constantly exhausted. Dr. Estés wrote, "When we are overdue for home, our eyes have nothing to sparkle for, our bones are weary, it is as though our nerve sheaths are unwrapped, and we can no longer focus on who or what we are about."[81] To be too far from that sense of home is to be overwhelmed by a longing that has turned into anger or numbness or bitterness or even rage. When we agree to, or are forced to, live our lives by approximation to the given ideal and the pre-made map, we often suffer great loss of home. This can be a spiritual, emotional, psychological, and/or physical exile. The obedient life runs the risk of being planted in the fabricated grids of colonized cultural gardens rather than in the soils of our own bodies, our own wildness, our own humanity. It is a life planted far from home.

Creative transgression has the power to guide us home. But there is no path. There is only the call in each moment to listen to our lives, to trust our bodies, to value our desires and longings. We listen to our bodies when they sing with the promise of pleasure and vibrate with the wonder of beauty, and we follow that song. It is to remember that we are not machines meant to live in the fantasy of uninterrupted growth, ascension, and productivity. It is to remember we are Nature. We are wild soft breathing pulsating hungering thirsting pleasuring dreaming creatures. We are not bad for being here fully. We are Home when we are here.

May we learn the art of growing down. May we learn to joyfully inhabit our bodies and be deeply rooted in the earth. May we revel in our belonging here.

# CURSES & COURAGE

*Behind naming, beneath words, is something else.*
*An existence named unnamed and unnameable...*
*And all this knowledge is in the souls of everything,*
*behind naming, before speaking, beneath words.*

**Susan Griffin**[82]

I grew up next to a small orphanage. As I remember it, the missionaries in our community started it when two abandoned young girls needed a home, and it grew from there. For most of my childhood the leader of the home was a charismatic and powerful woman whom I loved and respected. One day, a small group of us children were together in the community cafeteria and she walked in and solemnly asked us to gather around. *A curse has been cast,* she told us. And she named a young girl who lived in the orphanage, a girl I was friends with. They had found evidence of a Macumba curse ritual and somehow through the neighborhood web of concern had discovered that this particular young girl was the target of this curse. We all took it very seriously. She asked us to join her in prayer to ask for protection for the girl and to break the curse. We prayed together for a long time, sincerely and fervently. This was not out of place in the culture I grew up in. The invisible world was real. Not only because of the charismatic Christianity I was immersed in, but also because of the undercurrents of animism living just below the surface in much of Brazilian religious culture. Now I think of curses quite differently, but I am grateful to have been in a paradigm with so much space for wondering about the intangible mysteries we experience.

Many traditions and paradigms have their own way of imagining, recognizing, and enacting curses, these solemn utterances that harm. There are so many ways we have found to relate to the energetic forces shaping our lives, families, cultures, and societies. Some paradigms imagine them as spiritual entities affecting our world and our lives. Some imagine them as forces of Nature and biology that are not yet explained. Some imagine them as collective delusions. Some imagine them as invisible psychological forces with names like childhood wounds, attachment styles, and complexes. Some imagine them as archetypes. Some imagine them as astrological influences.

There are numerous unique and diverse ways of acknowledging and relating to the realities of the unseen world—realities that influence the contours of our lives, realities we sense and feel and but cannot concretely explain. I am often in wonder and astonishment at the power of imagination living through us. In the face of so much we don't understand, humans have found creative and beautiful ways of imagining our experiences here on Earth, in this galaxy, in this universe. We tell our stories and weave our meanings, even as we spin through space and time knowing there is a black hole at the center of the Milky Way that mercilessly takes matter and knowledge and will eventually disappear to a place we have not yet been able to imagine! In the presence of so much mystery, a life spent in wonder, reverence, and curiosity seems a more fitting and rational response than a life lived in certainty, dogma, and judgment.

In the way I think of it now, curses refer to those invisible, energetic, mythic forces shaping our lives that serve to keep us wounded, small, or lost. A curse is cast when a harmful story or a false name is given or taken—individually and collectively, personally and ancestrally. A curse is enacted when hatred is cast like an energetic shroud. A curse is lived out when a story of smallness and silence is planted and grows where largeness exists. A curse is woven when a prayer is said to make another into one's own image—in other words, when the person praying is using their energy and imagination in an attempt to make the other more like them or into what they want the other to be (beware of this, it is shadowy magic).

In the dream of the underground room, I came face to face with a profound personal and ancestral curse: live underground and make the most of it, and also, believe it is generous and be grateful. The dream was showing me a story; an invisible, though very real, force shaping the current of my life. Had I said yes and accepted that my fate was to make this haunted abandoned underground room as beautiful as possible, I would have given my life in service to a curse. I would have spent my life leaving my offerings at the altar of a story that served only to keep me busy with smallness and hiddenness, wondering all the while why I felt so wilted and unseen. This dream visited me as I was beginning my doctoral program, which in many ways was a transgressive act toward my own largeness. Transgression can act like a trip wire, bringing into visibility the curses that shape our lives.

When we enact a creative transgression, curses that have been unseen and unnamed (but most likely felt or sensed) become visible. Once our eyes are opened to the deeper realities of our lives, we begin to see the bargains and stories we are woven into. For example, when a child who lives in a paradisaical cocoon of parental praise steps into a vocation, religion, or sexual expression that the parents do not approve of, the bargain that had been invisible becomes visible. As they step beyond the approved way, they might learn that the bargain—the curse here—is that the child's life has been consecrated to the task of mirroring the parents. And once the child does not reflect the parents back to themselves Eden is over, and through that transgression, the life the child knew is over and something new must be created. Jung once wrote that "the greatest burden a child must bear is the unlived life of its parents."[83] We can imagine these burdens as curses, unconsciously binding and constraining the life of the child with stories, beliefs, and wounds that are not theirs. They become visible when they are transgressed. In the example above, if the child had never stepped beyond the approved way, the curse and constrictive bargain would likely have gone unseen and unnamed. Transgression helps us see, name, and move beyond the bad bargains and curses shaping our lives.

To stay in the Garden after knowing would be to live bound by curses. Once Eve transgressed, gained new knowledge, and became like the gods, Yahweh declared that her pain in childbirth would increase and that she would be ruled by her husband and her desire would be for him alone. Adam was cursed to have an antagonistic relationship with the land. The serpent was cursed to crawl on the Earth in a perpetual lowly position. Eve and the serpent were made to be enemies. Looked at symbolically, this curse speaks to the reality within Yahweh's Garden after the transgression. It speaks to staying after the knowing and reveals what it would cost to stay obedient after becoming like the gods.

The Eden story has cast a collective curse on our ways of being in the world. This idea that females are inferior and deserve punishment has been a centuries old curse that we carry individually, collectively, and generationally. The story that the Earth and humans exist in an antagonistic relationship, as Man is required to forcefully subdue the land into offering its nourishment, has had devastating impact on the ways we not only use the Earth as resource, but also in how we have been exiled from our deepest belonging as Nature. The image of the serpent—the oldest representation of the Goddess and a symbol for the cycles of death and rebirth, oracular knowing, and regeneration—being cast into the lowliest position and forced to crawl on its belly has been felt as the loss of connection and relationship with the ancient wisdom from these parts of Nature.

The image also shows us that when confronted by Yahweh, Adam blames Eve, and Eve blames the serpent. In order to survive within this paradigm after the transgression, the man turns on the woman, and the woman turns against the serpent. The binaries are not only cast in stone, the two sides are made to be at war with each other. Furthermore, there seems to be a deep truth buried here in the newly ordained relationship between the woman and the serpent, which is also reflected in the curse Yahweh pronounced upon the serpent, which included an "enmity between you and the woman."[84] In the new world—the one without Asherah—the woman's ancient and numinous relationship with the serpent would be severed. The serpent long symbolized the wisdom of the archetypal feminine sacred and those ways of being and knowing.

Symbolically, this suggests that what Yahweh is mandating is that Eve be forever severed from the feminine sacred and the sacrilization of the female. This is a profound violence, as Eve carries within herself the numinosity of Asherah and, therefore, is suddenly forced to sever herself from herself in order to live within this paradigm. In other words, in order for Eve to continue to live in the Garden after her eyes were opened would require her to turn on herself and on the ancient Nature wisdom the Goddess represents. It is as though the emerging paradigm shift required the suppression of these archetypal ways of being and knowing. It required a ruined female and an exiled Goddess.

These curses all paint a picture of what it means to live in Yahweh's Garden after the knowing, after the transgression. Even now, we live with these curses coursing through our lives, families, and societies. I imagine these as parts of the bargain we have to make in order to live in favor within patriarchal culture. In order to live in obedience to patriarchal ideologies, we must live with a denigrated female, an elevated male at war with the land, disconnected from the sacredness of the Earth and body, and severed from the ways of being and knowing associated with the images of the feminine sacred. We must turn on our ourselves and our inner knowing. As we question the status quo and trust our dis-ease with these bargains, these curses become more visible. As we transgress through seeing them, naming them, and challenging them, it often feels as if they are tightening and intensifying.

In the Eden story, it is almost as though, once Eve and Adam had seen the nature of their reality in the Garden, Yahweh had to place strict rules around their lives since, now, they had the capacity to discern and to understand their ability to choose something other than unconscious unity with Yahweh. Now they saw and they could question their obedience. Knowing and sovereignty—the ability to discern, choose, and be accountable for oneself—threaten paradigms that rely on obedience. Knowing and sovereignty threaten hierarchical systems of power-over. Living from the knowing of our bodies, our intuition, our dreams, and the Earth is an act of revolt that calls back what has been exiled for so long. It calls back aspects of our own sacredness as we re-member ourselves to ourselves and to Nature. The seeds break open and release the life that has been waiting in burial.

Transgression has the power to break curses.

The way of creative transgression requires courage. It is not easy to step beyond something that has named us, held us, and even fed us. When our eyes are opened to the curses in our lives, we need the courage to see, to tell the truth, to grieve, and when it is time, to transgress and reach.

# PERMISSION & TRUST

*When we don't listen to our intuition, we abandon our souls.*
*And we abandon our souls because we are afraid if we don't,*
*others will abandon us. We've been raised to question what we*
*know, to discount and discredit the authority of our gut.*

**Terry Tempest Williams**[85]

At great cost, Eve follows her inner law step by step, moving from one experience and revelation to the next. She finds her way not through willful effort toward a predestined goal but through the body, through the more-than-human world, through intuition, and through desire. This is a way of inquiry and quest that is not motivated by a destination but by an inner call and impulse to know, regardless of consequence. It is a commitment to taking the next step, not knowing where you are going or what you will find. It is a labyrinthine dance of taking the next step, then the next. Imagine if Eve had heard the truth in the serpent's council and seen that the fruit was good for knowing, beauty, and nourishment and then, before taking the next step, she had sought permission from Yahweh to reach for the forbidden fruit. Eve did not only see and desire. She also trusted what she saw and what she desired, and because of that trust she reached. At that threshold she did not look to Yahweh for permission, instead she became the source of her own inner permission.

I have noticed that often what we call problems of knowing are actually problems of permission. I often sit down with folks who are looking for their knowing. As we slow down and listen, it becomes evident that the knowing is already unmistakably there—*I want to go back to school, I don't want this job, this relationship is costing me too much, I need to move, speak up, slow down, wait...* Quickly, we discover that what we are looking for is not the knowing, it is the permission to move and live according to that knowing. We can have deep knowing, but if we don't find the permission to enact and embody that knowing we remain split. We remain in the obedient life, suffering the fate of a dissonant existence. In this situation, the inner vision is not in harmony with the ways we live our days. Inner permission is the bridge between deep knowing and the life you are living in the world.

The Latin roots of the word *permission* mean "through" and "to send and let go," "to grant liberty." While transgression is a stepping across a set boundary, permission is the force at the center of the mandate that releases its hold and allows one to cross over into a new way of being. Permission must be found in order to cross over from the center of a *should* into creative transgression. Sometimes this is found consciously and other times unconsciously, but something has to loosen in order for us to break the bonds of obedience to a familiar way.

In order to move from a life of blind obedience into a life of sovereignty, we must learn to honestly ask the question: *Where am I looking to for permission to live from my own knowing?* This is a very important question because if you are still looking to the old authorities to grant you the liberty to transgress, you may become stuck in a dissonant space between what you know and how you live. It is most likely that you will never find permission from the places you are disobeying. They will not grant it. You will have to find your permission somewhere else.

Asking the question of where you look to for permission will also guide you into seeing who has power over your life. Consciously and curiously exploring these questions of permission in your life is a crucial part of finding more freedom to live from your wild knowing. How much energy are you spending convincing those you are disobeying that your knowing and reaching are valid? How much time are you devoting to waiting for blessing from the very authorities (inner or outer) that you are transgressing?

Permission from external authorities is the scaffolding of the obedient life. Inner permission is at the heart of sovereignty. To violate the boundaries of another's permission, stealing away their right to grant permission over their own bodies, spirits, hearts, minds, is to violate their innate sovereignty. Abuse of permission is a violent abuse of power. And yet, it can be so easy to give away our permission.

Here we find one of the most compelling traps of leaving the obedient life for the knowing life. It will be tempting to simply transfer that power of permission to another source outside of yourself, rather than taking the bold risk of falling fully into your inner permission. In other words, it is easy to replace one paradigm of obedience with another, to replace one punishing god for another.

For example, in our quest to end the patriarchal age we might long to replace God/maleness with Goddess/femaleness as the highest authority. Or instead of religious doctrine we might look to therapeutic dogma to rule our lives, casting off an ideal of salvation for an ideal of health or wellness. Hierarchical and monotheistic styles of thinking are deeply ingrained in the Western consciousness and, if we are not awake to questions of permission, we may simply exchange one obedient life after the other, never actually descending into trusting ourselves as our own authority.

The very paradigms that have upheld the warning that we are not trustworthy as sources of knowing, permission, and blessing are precisely the paradigms that benefit from our lack of trust in ourselves. This has been a vicious and effective cycle.

I have sat with many people who are asking a variation of this question: *After so long of not trusting my own heart and body, so long being continually told to not trust myself, how do I trust myself again?* Of course, I have also often wondered this in my own life—often daily. I think it is a lifelong labor. And I have found that embracing a slightly different question has offered more spaciousness in this labor.

Trust in relationship is not only built on the big moments or lofty promises. Yes, those are important. But what we are learning more and more is that trust is mostly built in the small moments, in small promises made and kept. Showing up on time. Remembering significant days. Paying attention and making time for the other. Believing each other. Those small moments have an incredible impact on trust in a relationship. Although trust can be destroyed in a moment, it is built over time with the slow and steady braiding of intention, attention, and action.

Sometimes we can stand frozen before this monolithic question: *How do I trust myself?* The question is so large, the history is so deep and muddled. Perhaps it may be more fruitful to ask each morning: *How can I build trust with myself today?* Rather than imagining a miraculous shift into unwavering trust, we can imagine a few small steps, a few small promises we can keep that day. We can turn loving attention to our hearts and bodies and vow to pay attention—and then pay attention later that day when someone casts words that wound and instead of telling yourself *toughen-up-they-didn't-mean-it-like-that-you-are-too-sensitive* stories, find a quiet enough space, take a deep breath, place your hand on your heart, and reassure your being: *I see you and your hurt; I love you; I will never leave you.* Begin small. Think of how you would coax a small wild animal into trusting you. Gentle. Steady. Kind. And slowly the bridge you are building gets stronger and stronger.

As you invite your heart and body to speak, they will be making bids for trust. As you listen in small ways, the trust will strengthen. It can be as simple as listening to your body and eating when you are hungry instead of eating simply when it is time to eat. Or as simple as resting when you are tired (naps are one of my favorite transgressive spiritual practices!). Maybe your heart is nudging you to reach out to a friend and you call. Or maybe your body is asking you to say no to something and you stay home. As you increase this dialogue in the mutual reassurance of intention, attention, and action, you are weaving a life of trust.

I imagine that if Eve had stopped in the moment of her knowing and looked to Yahweh for permission, she would not have reached for the forbidden fruit. She may have waited her whole mythic life in that Garden, living obediently. Maybe she eventually would have started training others to not be deceived by the serpent, by the beauty of the fruit, by the longing for nourishment, or by the danger of desire. I imagine her walking with more and more stiffness and rigidity as she paced the bounds of obedience and favor.

Would the favor have begun to taste sour in her mouth as she dreamed of the sweet flesh of the fruit on her lips, its juices trickling down her neck? Would the well-worn path have brought the comfort of familiarity or the restlessness of a caged animal? I imagine wistfulness in her eyes as she looked perpetually to the horizon for a life that made sense. I imagine that sometimes, in the quiet between night and day, she would feel the full force of her knowing and longing and realize that she would be willing to give up all the calm, favor, and blessing in order to taste that fruit. *Someday*, I imagine her saying to herself, *maybe someday.*

# THE BLESSING BONE

*When I get stuck in painful emotions, it brings me to a repeating realization, an insight that has profoundly changed my life:* I have to love myself into healing. *The only path that can carry me home is the path of self-compassion.*

**Tara Brach**[86]

When I began to follow the questions and longings that were unfurling themselves and breaking down the containers that had held me, I also began to lose the blessing of my community and of my elders. I could no longer be the dutiful daughter, the selfless martyr, and the devoted follower. I wanted to be those things, in many ways. But I couldn't. And the loss felt unbearable sometimes. For years I grappled with the loss of blessing from my community. I walked out without their permission. I walked out with my own permission. But then I found myself wandering in a land I did not know, without favor and without blessing. I walked wounded, with stories of shame and cruelty blowing against me like powerful gales trying to push me back into obedience.

In those slow years, I didn't rage at anyone but myself. I didn't burn it all down. I didn't speak my truth from the rooftops. I didn't confront anyone. I retreated. I tried to disappear into a safer place until I was stronger, until I knew what was even happening. I walked very quietly out of the Garden into the unknown. This was not a conscious choice; it was all I could do. I was still too 'good' to confront or hurt anyone, so I turned on myself. I only know that now, looking back. Sometimes, it can feel so much easier to turn on ourselves first. Sometimes, it can feel so right to choose to protect the stories we have been devoted to, rather than to fight for our own lives.

But I kept walking. It took years of exhaustion and slow loss until I finally began to sense a new form and a new way of being. It took years until I finally began to see little signs of rebirth instead of only feeling the grief of death. It took years for me to begin to find a blessing that came from a much deeper and older place than from the beautiful but shallow pools of my obedience.

Bound up in the questions of permission are also the questions of blessing. In other words, where we look to for permission is often where we look to for blessing, where we look to for that assurance that we are loved and worthy from the gaze that bestows favor. When we transgress the approved boundaries of obedience, not only will we stop receiving permission from those old places of authority, we also can expect to lose their blessing. This often propels us into a profoundly disorienting crisis of blessing. The usual places we have looked to for favor, encouragement, acceptance, and belonging will no longer offer us these. And very often, they will offer messages of rejection and shame instead. This can be a devastating experience. Not only are we then left with the mythic task of finding and trusting our own permission, we will also be called to search for our blessing and belonging in deeper and truer places.

Years ago, I attended a training with one of my most important teachers. She often speaks of the vows we make before we are born—vows toward our own souls and fates. I find this to be a beautiful way to imagine our lives, sometimes, as we deepen into the mysterious forces shaping our lives. During this training I was so aware as she talked about the vows that, for me, keeping those vows toward my own life had meant a profound loss of blessing from my elders. And I was filled with a longing so deep and fierce it was painful. I wanted my birthright blessing from this teacher. I was filled with a desperate hunger to no longer wander without deep blessing.

There were over one hundred people at this training and access to the teacher was almost impossible. But during a break, I saw another trainee speaking with her so I thought I could approach her and do the same. As I approached her someone stepped between us and said no, I could not talk with her now. I stood there watching another speak freely with her while I was barred from what I thought I needed most. It felt hauntingly familiar. In that frozen moment, all the yearning, rejection, exile, and loss came rushing up from my center like a flood. I thought I would dissolve in its wake. I was denied blessing even as I watched another receive and be nurtured. Why was I sent away, again? I felt the weeping rattling my defenses and used all my strength to walk through the crowd and out the door. I was embarrassed to be feeling so much after a seemingly small incident. I managed to get outside to my favorite grove under some trees, looking over a meadow, and I wept. I wept when I got back to my room that night. I was so full of longing, and the longing was turning into rage. I let it be there with me, doing its work.

The next morning, I still felt heartbroken but calmer. As I moved through that next day of training, I knew something deep in my bones: the blessing I needed could not come from that teacher. The blessing I was looking for had to come from a deeper place. I was denied because I had to keep wandering into the heart of my spiritual exile in order to find the blessing that would not fade—my birthright blessing. Later, in ceremony, this vision came to me and I wrote it into a story called "The Blessing Bone":

*Once upon a time I was a very good girl.*

*I was so obedient that I could not see or name the harsh environs where I lived. I called it good. I did not yet know my birthright blessing had been stolen. Since there were no true mirrors, I could not see who I was or who I was meant to be.*

*One day I heard a call. I heard the voice of a god drawing me into the forest, past the depths, across the boundary I was forbidden to cross. But, recognizing God's voice and believing I would find nourishment, I followed the call into the forbidden forest. And there, instead of nourishment I found the body of my dead God.*

*I wept.*

*I went missing for ten years. For ten years I tended the body until it turned to bones. I buried the bones properly in sacred ritual.*

*I did not know who I was or what I was to do. I could see now that my birthright blessing was lost, or stolen, but I could not find it. I did not know where to look. I could barely move. Until one day, a beautiful woman appeared before me.*

*"Your sorrow drew me here. Your tears showed me the way and sustained me on my journey. Your insistence on your sorrow has brought me to you," she said. "I am Lady Death and I have come to give you something you need."*

*Before I could speak, she thrust her hand into my chest and reached into the darkest corner of my heart and for a moment it stopped. For a moment I was dead. I looked into her eyes and I was not afraid. My heart began to beat again, but with a new rhythm, her rhythm.*

*Lady Death handed me a small blessing bundle.*

*"This is your birthright blessing, I buried it, right here, in your heart long ago."*

*I opened the small bundle, unwinding the rope. In the small center of the bundle I found the smallest bone of my dead God. And on that bone, written in tiny careful script, I read my vow, my truest wordless name.*

*This was my blessing bone. My birthright, the blessing I had lost and now found.*

*"I miss God," I told her.*

*"Turn around," she said as she turned my shoulders.*

*Like Eve, my eyes were suddenly opened, and I saw that while I had wept, the bones of God had become something new. The uneven contours of the earth Her curvy flesh. The rustling leaves Her hair. The trees and roots Her limbs, reaching toward the edges and pressing toward the center. The flowers Her fragrance. The birds Her song.*

*I had always longed for Her. And now I knew Her.*

*My heart was full, and I saw Her.*

*We had long years of quiet communion in the woods, for the village would not take me back.*

*"Will I ever go back?" I asked Lady Death one day. "I miss the elders. Who will sing to me when I am lonely?"*

*"Listen!" she said, "Look!"*

*And I began to hear one, two, a chorus of voices singing from time and from a place outside of time. My heart pulsated to the rhythm of The Song and I felt the Deep Rhythm.*

*Just at that moment a slanted stream of sunlight fell across my face and I remembered the old story of a resurrected wolf that turned into a woman. Now I had seen with my own eyes and felt in my own heart the terror, the power, the creation, the destruction constantly swirling through the Holy Mysteries.*

*And I knew in my bones that although I may feel alone, I would never be alone.*

*"Make trails. Leave peace offerings. Tell new stories," Lady Death told me. "Go do your work."*

# UNKNOWING & THE UNKNOWN

*The dance is always danced above the hollow
place, above the terrible abyss.*

**Ursula Le Guin**[87]

I wonder often about this paradox: the beating heart of a knowing
life is unknowing. Making peace with the Unknown is necessary
if we are to step beyond—or at least begin to question—the maps
and directions we have been given for our lives. The dark generative
fertility of unknowing is the womb required for the creation of consciousness. Learning to bow down to the permeating presence of the
Unknown in our lives creates the space from which new knowing
can emerge.

If everything is known and we have no questions, only answers,
there is little opportunity for new life to push through the walls
of our certainty—it can, but usually does so less frequently and in
much more destructive ways. We have a gentler freedom to know
new things in new ways when we admit unknowing and develop a
friendly attitude towards the Unknown. All knowing emerges out
of the dark womb of what is unknown, unconscious, and unseen.
We inhabit the Unknown. We can witness this through our mythic
sensibility, our spiritual intuition, our psychological observations,
and our scientific inquiry.

Carl Jung's theory of the objective psyche offers us an imagination of how the known dialogues with the unknown. He imagined
a transpersonal psyche that includes both a personal unconscious

consisting of each person's specific stories, wounds or complexes, and shadows, and a collective unconscious consisting of universal patterns and dynamics, i.e., archetypes. For Jung, individuation happens when what is known is transformed by what is unknown, that is, our consciousness is expanded and transformed as it deepens relationship with the less illuminated life of the deep psyche. In this process the unconscious is also transformed.[88] The idea is that our consciousness is held and exists within a vast collective psyche which exists mostly beyond the small illuminated circle of our conscious awareness. In other words, it is unconscious to us. The unconscious is not a place, it surrounds us and lives within us.

The unconscious cannot be seen directly but its effects can be felt. This is how we came to name the psychological experience of the archetypal unconscious—we know it exists through its effects, the same way we know a wind is blowing through a forest because of how the trees sway. We cannot see the wind, but we observe what it touches, moves, and shapes. This is reminiscent of apophatic theology: a way of knowing God through what cannot be said or seen. Apophatic theology is also known as negative theology: the divine is named by not naming and through absence. The mystery is sensed not by what is present but by what cannot be present. There are many ways we circle around the mysterious reality that there is much we sense and feel but cannot see or know directly.

Sometime during the years leading up to that Tuesday, I found myself in the Colorado mountains gazing into inky blue skies adorned with thousands of small hollows of light, like portals into another world. Vastness was a tangible presence. As I inhabited the Vastness that night, my eyes were opened to this: the mysteries were immeasurably larger than the confines of the God I had been serving. The religion was a container that could sometimes dispense the mysteries in small meaningful increments, but it could never contain the mysteries. On that particular night, this thought came to me as the realization that God was not a Christian. I don't mean that I think God can't be found in Christianity; I mean that I viscerally felt that whatever I had called God was not contained there. I realized that though I had experienced God within those walls in true and beautiful ways, the mystery I called God could never be held *only* there. And didn't I want to know God, to know truth, to know what's real? How could I not acknowledge that beyond the small illuminated circle of what I had been taught was a vast Unknowing where God *also* existed? On that night, it was that God who showed me that I would have to choose whether I would follow the truth of my lived experience and my questions or stay within the confines of that One Way. It was that God who became the seeds of my new life, even as he died on that Tuesday, and later returned in new ways and with new names and in an ever-shifting cacophony of multiplicity and mystery.

Many have told me that I have left God, some even that they don't see God in me, that I have gone astray, that I have never known what it means to walk with God. But I now trust this: that childhood God led me to the edges of the approved life and said, *Go follow your own knowing.* That night in Colorado, I suddenly knew I would have to follow the mysteries out of the boundaries that had been given to me, I would have to wander beyond the approved truth, the prescribed life, in order to be true to what was calling me—a calling I could not name but only feel. Rigid walls of certainty became porous. The *I know* at the center of my life became a terrifying and liberating *I don't know.*

The words, *I don't know* have the power to disarm rigid and exclusionary paradigms. They can crack open too small containers that were crafted in certainty and rely on unquestioned obedience to that One Truth. To walk through life in the posture of *I don't know* allows us to sit in the face of something we do not understand, do not like, and even maybe don't agree with and *still find the ability to offer the experience dignity and honor.*

When we live with a deep reverence for the Unknowing at the heart of our existence, the other does not have to be made evil. The other can have space to be sacred and true, even if we don't understand it—whether we are speaking of a person, a group of people, a worldview, or experiences in our own hearts, minds, spirits, and bodies. Carrying reverence for the unknown creates a space large enough for our multiplicity to be held in true dignity and kinship.

Truth with a capital "T" leaves no room for unknowing. As we slowly learn to break down the One Truth into the many truths inherent in the multiplicity of lived experience, the existential terror—and often the fury of religious fervor—arrives with intensity and with swift punishment. Many, especially in fundamentalist religious paradigms, have considered this a breakdown of Reality itself, rather than a shattering of the One perspective into the many perspectives.

I grew up being taught that doubt, not knowing, and uncertainty were a sign of the weakness of the beholder and insult to Reality. In that context, to say my truth may be different than your truth was a commentary of reality itself, rather than an acknowledgment that we see and experience that reality from different perspectives and from within a cloud of unknowing. In other words, the idea of many truths was an insult to God himself, rather than a humble acknowledgement of our limitations and diversities as beholders. The deeper and further I live into this mystery of living, breathing, meaning making, loving, losing, and dying, the more the posture of unknowing and wonder seem like the most sane response.

To befriend the Unknown is to find a continual posture of bowing down to a reality that far exceeds our ability to consciously understand it. Yes, the unknown can be and often is scary, even terrifying. And it is a relief. It is both the terrible abyss over which we dance our lives, and it is the grace that softens the edges of this liminal incarnation. To befriend the Unknown is to live in wonder, rather than certainty in the face of mysteries we can only circle over and over again. I can have strong feelings and intricate opinions about things. I can fight fiercely for what I believe in. I can live passionately and wholeheartedly. And I can live with the knowing that the still point of the dance is a deep bow of humility to the truth that I don't know—that is the grace and relief of dancing, loving, living, and losing above the great and terrible abyss of Unknowing.

# AT THE CENTER OF YOUR OWN CIRCLE

*Give me to do everything I do in the day*
*with a sense of the sacredness of life.*

**May Sarton**[89]

At the end of the first year of the global pandemic as I grappled with grief over what had been lost and what was going to be lost in my life, I practiced the ritual of the death lodge for two months.[90] For those weeks I lightened my work load and during the time I had to myself I would go to my little hut in the woods and sit. I would meditate, imagine, and be with my life just as it was. I sat with the truths growing from me like wild weeds disrupting the tame and cultivated places of my life. I sat with the grief and sadness of loss. I sat with the fear of annihilation. I was realizing and accepting that my marriage of over twenty years was ending. I sat with the rage of disappointment. At the end of these two months I went on a solitary retreat for eight days.

I rented a sweet tiny house on an island in the Puget Sound. It was a beautiful little spot with an outdoor shower and trails in the woods. I walked. I rested. The sleeping loft had skylights, so at night I could watch the moon. Mostly I sat on a little bench by the window and watched the hummingbirds come to a feeder throughout the day. I decided I would not effort. I would just be there, watching and waiting, like someone sitting next to a pond calmly watching what might come up to the surface. When things came up, I would write, meditate, pray, process. And otherwise, I was just there.

On the last day of the retreat, I sat at the window again, a fire burning in the tiny wood stove. I went into the ceremony of descending into the mystical and imaginal realm (another practice and experience for which many traditions have numerous and diverse names). I saw myself sitting at the pond, watching. And what I saw come to the surface of the waters was gruesome and beautiful.

I saw my previous self, young and beautiful, float to the top of the pond, face down. I immediately knew who she was, and it was hard not to look away. But slowly I pulled her out of the waters, and I was filled with profound love and shattering grief. How brave and beautiful she was! How strong and true! I took her to the foot of a great tree and adorned her body with flowers and things of nature. In my body I felt an almost indescribable love for her, a deep gratitude for all she had been through to get me here. I spent time with her outside of time in ritual burial. Her life had been remarkable. And now a new one was beginning.

I left that day to face the hardest year of my life so far. That year I would face the end of my marriage and profound changes in my family. It was almost unimaginable; it was devastating. The act of re-imagining and allowing our family to take new form took away the ground I stood on and I had to, once again, let my life fall through. There were many times when I felt I would not survive the grief and fear and sadness. But thankfully, grief is like the tides. Its rhythms of coming and going carve out new spaces in our inner shores and we become able to hold more.

I left that day filled with a deep love for my own life that has not left me. I don't mean that I have liked my life. I mean that even when I thought I would probably never like my life again, I loved this wild gift that was given to me.

Eve sacrificed much for knowing, for beauty, for nourishment, and for pleasure. She lost favor. She lost the quiet of an unexamined life. She lost the ease of obedience and easy answers. To sacrifice means to make sacred. What we sacrifice has to do with what we consecrate our lives to. A powerful way to clearly see what your life is devoted to is to name honestly what you are sacrificing. It is also wise to wonder who is choosing your sacrifices. Who is choosing what your life is in service to? Often, in a life of unexamined obedience we are not the ones choosing what we sacrifice. And so, we are not the ones choosing what our lives are consecrated to. We can discern the gods and goddesses we worship by noticing whose altar we leave offerings on.

Maybe you make sacrifices of financial stability in order to spend more time with your art. Maybe for years you choose a job you don't enjoy so that you can have a more comfortable retirement. Maybe you forgo the social abundance of the city to live closer to the natural world. This isn't about right or wrong. It is about what you are rendering sacred in your life. It is about what you are valuing above other things. It is about what you are spending your visible and invisible resources on.

In an obedient life, as in the Garden of Eden, the bargain for living in favor is the relinquishment of seeing and knowing. In other words, we often sacrifice seeing and knowing in exchange for the promise of safety, belonging, and ease. Creative transgressions out of these bargains often result in the sacrifice of the sense of belonging and safety, for a time. When our eyes are opened to the ways of Nature, we see that sacrifice is always required. When we choose one thing, another is not chosen. The liberating question, then, is not: *Will there be sacrifice?* but rather, *Which sacrifices and who is choosing them?*

Sovereignty—to be self-belonging and self-governing—is weighty. It is not only the ecstasy of remembering ourselves and our belonging and our power. It is also the knowing that we are strong enough to hold the consequence of choice. It is the courage to stand at the center of our own circles as the sources of our knowing, permission, and blessing. It is the courage to stand at the center of our own circles holding the weight of our freedom. When we have a demanding god or goddess (be that a religious image, a collective imperative, an inner voice, or a family figure) as the source of our instructions, we hand over both power and also accountability. We can shake our fists at those gods (of Christianity, Capitalism, Atheism, Wellness, etc.) and blame them for not giving us knowing or for causing us to choose badly. To be sovereign is to have no one to tell you what to do and also to have no one to blame. We sacrifice martyrdom for sovereignty.

When we stand at the center of our own circle, we are creating worlds. What if we remember the powers of creation and destruction live in the same space? That light and dark, growth and decay, death and rebirth all live in Nature, in us, in the Mysteries? When the images of the goddesses were exiled and buried and their stories largely forbidden in the world, their wisdom was severed from our memory. They were the carriers of this deep knowing, this sacred truth: *it all belongs.* To remember them is to re-member ourselves into our fullness and belonging.

To stand at the center of our own circles is to name ourselves, to hold our power to create and to destroy with reverence, to invoke blessing wherever possible and to be careful not to cast curses since we know we are One Flesh. To stand at the center of our own circle is to seek our blessing in wild Nature rather than in the construct of culture. To stand at the center of our own circle is to trust our bodies as sacred instinctual sexual spiritual powerful oracular precious creatures full of knowing. To stand at the center of our own circle is to have the courage to look and not look away.

Our eyes are opened. We see through the surface of things and trust our own knowing, even as we remain deeply connected in the web of our belonging.

Draw your circles, friends.

Stand at the center.

Create new worlds.

# EPILOGUE

*The Goddess is the unspeakable wisdom that grows into the very cells of the body. She lives with this sacramental truth at her center: the beauty and the horror of the whole of life are blazing in Her love. She is dancing in the flames.*

**Marion Woodman and Elinor Dickson**[91]

Since I started writing this book, I have been through many transitions. More transgressions. More unraveling. This seems to be the way of the knowing life, a life that lives by its own compass rather than by a predesigned map. It is a life that is constantly remade. Continually done and undone, stitched and unstitched, told and untold and retold.

I am not here telling you that this way of creative transgression away from the shoulds and into your own knowing—whatever that may mean for you today—is going to make you happier, more enlightened, better, or healthier. In fact, it is more likely to make you muddier and messier. It may make living in culture harder. It may cause you to have less success within the paradigms of capitalism. You may grow up, but you will also grow down.

This book isn't meant to be about self-improvement. It is written as an ode to the wild. The wild that calls us to learn to live more freely in our nature. To believe in our beauty and inherent worth, rather than in a poisonous tale of our fallenness and depravity. To challenge the hierarchical systems of power-over that sever us not only from ourselves, but from each other and from the earth, systems that create injustice and enact unspeakable violence. This work is meant as a song in praise of our humanity as a part of the sacred mystery of all things. It is meant as an invocation of blessing over our fullness and belonging.

I don't know if my life is better or worse for all the transgressions out of the approved and favored places. Those are not words that belong in the wild. Their measurements and evaluations are not relevant here because they require intricate systems of hierarchy in order to work. They require a vision of wholeness through approximation to one ideal image rather than wholeness through the inclusion of the many.[92]

I can say there is more hardship and more ease. More tears and more joy. More sorrow and more wonder. More loneliness and more belonging. What I do know is that it is freer and truer. What I do know is that I have never loved my life more. I don't mean my life as a product or commodity but as a living tender wild creature given to my stewardship. I have a deeper friendship with myself than I could have imagined. And because of that, I think I can offer the people in my life and the land I live on more love and more friendship.

I have the practice of imagining my deathbed self. I imagine the moment we will meet there at that place of transition, another place of transgression beyond what is known into what is unknown. Birth and Death stand as two thresholds of transgression that create a space where we get to experience life on this exquisite earth, in these wonderous bodies. In this way, all of life is liminal. As I imagine her, I sense it would be a great tragedy to meet her there and know I had not loved well the life I was given. To know that I had not really been here. To know I had not deeply and lovingly participated in the mystery of this liminal incarnation.

I may not be better or healthier or more enlightened.

But I am more here.

I am here.

# APPENDIX

## Genesis Text (New International Version)

*Now the serpent was more crafty than any of the wild animals the Lord God had made.*

*He said to the woman, "Did God really say, 'You must not eat from any tree in the garden'?"*

*The woman said to the serpent, "We may eat fruit from the trees in the garden, but God did say, 'You must not eat fruit from the tree that is in the middle of the garden, and you must not touch it, or you will die.'"*

*"You will not certainly die," the serpent said to the woman. "For God knows that when you eat from it your eyes will be opened, and you will be like God, knowing good and evil."*

*When the woman saw that the fruit of the tree was good for food and pleasing to the eye, and also desirable for gaining wisdom, she took some and ate it. She also gave some to her husband, who was with her, and he ate it.*

*Then the eyes of both of them were opened, and they realized they were naked; so they sewed fig leaves together and made coverings for themselves.*

*Then the man and his wife heard the sound of the Lord God as he was walking in the garden in the cool of the day, and they hid from the Lord God among the trees of the garden.*

*But the Lord God called to the man, "Where are you?"*

*He answered, "I heard you in the garden, and I was afraid because I was naked; so I hid."*

*And he said, "Who told you that you were naked? Have you eaten from the tree that I commanded you not to eat from?"*

*The man said, "The woman you put here with me—she gave me some fruit from the tree, and I ate it."*

*Then the Lord God said to the woman, "What is this you have done?"*

*The woman said, "The serpent deceived me, and I ate."*

*So the Lord God said to the serpent, "Because you have done this,*

*"Cursed are you above all livestock and all wild animals! You will crawl on your belly and you will eat dust all the days of your life. And I will put enmity between you and the woman, and between your offspring and hers; he will crush your head, and you will strike his heel."*

*To the woman he said, "I will make your pains in childbearing very severe; with painful labor you will give birth to children. Your desire will be for your husband, and he will rule over you."*

*To Adam he said, "Because you listened to your wife and ate fruit from the tree about which I commanded you, 'You must not eat from it,'*

*"Cursed is the ground because of you; through painful toil you will eat food from it all the days of your life. It will produce thorns and thistles for you, and you will eat the plants of the field. By the sweat of your brow you will eat your food until you return to the ground, since from it you were taken; for dust you are and to dust you will return."*

*Adam named his wife Eve, because she would become the mother of all the living.*

*The Lord God made garments of skin for Adam and his wife and clothed them. And the Lord God said, "The man has now become like one of us, knowing good and evil. He must not be allowed to reach out his hand and take also from the tree of life and eat, and live forever." So the Lord God banished him from the Garden of Eden to work the ground from which he had been taken. After he drove the man out, he placed on the east side of the Garden of Eden cherubim and a flaming sword flashing back and forth to guard the way to the tree of life.*

# ACKNOWLEDGMENTS

*In a voiced community, we all flourish.*

**Terry Tempest Williams**[93]

I am astonished by the beautiful dance of giving and receiving love and support as we unfurl ourselves into the world. During the writing of this book, I have received that love and support in so many ways: brave and loving questions, words of encouragement, keen-eyed editing, hours of deep listening, last minute childcare, nourishing dinners, honest feedback, intellectual inquiry, thoughtful celebrations, shared tears, and even more words of encouragement. It all feels miraculous to me. I am filled with gratitude for all that has been given during the writing of this book.

Thank you to Lucy Pearce and the Womancraft Publishing team for choosing to bring this book into the world. It is a profound honor to be a part of the Womancraft community.

I have also been deeply honored to spend so many of my days accompanying courageous folks as they listen to their lives, cultivate inner friendship, and move deeper into wild knowing. I have learned so much as we have walked through dark pathless forests, adventured to the underworld, explored bewildering dreams, listened to the songs of the soul, and braved the Wild together. This book has been significantly enriched through our work together. And my life is continually enriched through our work together. Thank you.

I have had wonderful teachers and guides along the way. I want to especially thank Dr. Thomas Moore for introducing me to the care of the soul and the archetypal way so many years ago. I am so grateful for your perspective and wisdom. Your support has been very meaningful to me. Thank you.

I am deeply grateful for my close community, the ecology of my belonging—friends, family, animals, land. Natalie, Liz, Ava, Laura, Karolina, and Cherie—the love and support you have offered me over these years of writing have truly made this book possible. You each show me in your own ways what it means to be brave, knowing, and wild. So much of what I have learned about this mythic journey I have learned from you. Thank you.

Ash, being your mother is the most beautiful miracle I have experienced in this life. You are a brilliant, creative, and brave soul. Thank you for showing me so much about what it means to be here. Watching you become more and more yourself as you learn how to stand at the center of your own circle is one of the greatest joys of my life. I am endlessly grateful for you.

And I offer my gratitude to Eve, who stirs at the threshold between obedience and desire, between knowing and unknowing, between the safe life and the unexpected life, between domesticity and wildness, and where the deepest longing of our hearts threatens worlds. She found me there, and I will always be grateful.

# ENDNOTES

1.  Beverly Lanzetta. *Radical Wisdom: A Feminist Mystical Theology.*

2.  John Phillips. *Eve: The History of an Idea.*

3.  This is my own retelling of the events of the creation myth found in *Genesis*. The events in the Garden are in the original text. In the second half of the story, I go deeper and bring in the mythological and imaginal context of the myth, rooted in years of scholarly research into the mythological belonging and psycho-spiritual meaning of this story. For the original text see the Appendix.

4.  Sue Monk Kidd. *The Dance of the Dissident Daughter: A Woman's Journey from Christian Tradition to the Sacred Feminine.*

5.  Clarissa Pinkola Estés. *The Faithful Gardener: A Wise Tale About That Which Can Never Die.*

6.  Fritjof Capra. *The Turning Point: Science, Society, and the Rising Culture.*

7.  For more on this see Joseph Cambray, *Synchronicity: Nature and Psyche in an Interconnected Universe* and Fritof Kapra, *The Turning Point.*

8.  Joseph Cambray. *Synchronicity: Nature and Psyche in an Interconnected Universe.*

9.  Robin Wall Kimmerer. *Braiding Sweetgrass: Indigenous Wisdom, Scientific Knowledge, and the Teaching of Plants.*

10. A term coined by David Abram in *Spell of the Sensuous: Perception and Language in a More-Than-Human World.*

11. Marie Louise von Franz. *Creation Myths.*

12. Robin Wall Kimmerer. *Braiding Sweetgrass: Indigenous Wisdom, Scientific Knowledge, and the Teaching of Plants.*

13. Carl Jung. *The Archetypes and the Collective Unconscious.*

14. Thomas Moore. "Developing a Mythic Sensibility."

15. I learned this phrase from Dr. Glen Slater.

16. Rafael Patai. *The Hebrew Goddess.*

17. Mary Daly. *Beyond God the Father: Toward a Philosophy of Women's Liberation.*

18. Christine Downing. *The Goddess: Mythological Images of the Feminine.*

19. Esther Harding. *Woman's Mysteries Ancient and Modern.*

20. Christine Downing. *The Goddess: Mythological Images of the Feminine.*

21. Merlin Stone. *When God was a Woman.*

22. For example, see Robin Wall Kimmerer's beautiful account of Skywoman in her book, *Braiding Sweetgrass.*

23. Arthur George and Elena George. *The Mythology of Eden*

24. For example, see *I Kings* 14:15; *I Kings* 14: 16; *2 Kings* 17: 7-18; *I Kings* 16:33; *I Kings* 18:19; *2 Kings* 13:6; *Judges* 3:7.

25. Arthur George and Elena George. *The Mythology of Eden*

26. Rafael Patai. *The Hebrew Goddess.*

27. Rafael Patai. *The Hebrew Goddess.*

28. Anne Baring and Jules Cashford. *Myth of the Goddess: Evolution of an Image.*

29. Arthur George and Elena George. *The Mythology of Eden*

30. Arthur George and Elena George. *The Mythology of Eden*

31. Arthur George and Elena George. *The Mythology of Eden*

32. Arthur George and Elena George. *The Mythology of Eden*

33. Anne Baring and Jules Cashford. *Myth of the Goddess: Evolution of an Image* and Arthur George and Elena George. *The Mythology of Eden*

34. Arthur George and Elena George. *The Mythology of Eden*

35. Merlin Stone. *When God was a Woman.*

36. Christine Downing. *The Goddess: Mythological Images of the Feminine.*

37. Terry Tempest Williams. *When Women Were Birds: Fifty-Four Variations on Voice.*

38. James Hillman. "Betrayal."

39. John O'Donohue. "For the Interim Time."

40. John O'Donohue. "For the Interim Time."

41. Mary Oliver. "Starfish."

42. Marion Woodman. *Coming Home to Myself: Reflections for Nurturing a Woman's Body and Soul.*

43. James Hollis. *What Matters Most: Living a More Considered Life.*

44. Toko-pa Turner. *Belonging: Remembering Ourselves Home.*

45. James Sprenger and Heinrich Kramer. *Malleus Malificarum.*

46. James Sprenger and Heinrich Kramer. *Malleus Malificarum.*

47. David Whyte. *Crossing the Unknown Sea: Work as a Pilgrimage of Identity.*

48. Naomi Replansky. "Housing Shortage."

49. Clarissa Pinkola Estés. *Women Who Run with the Wolves: Myths and Stories of the Wild Woman Archetype.*

50. Mary Daly. *Beyond God the Father: Toward a Philosophy of Women's Liberation.*

51. Mary Daly. *Beyond God the Father: Toward a Philosophy of Women's Liberation.*

52. Merlin Stone. *When God was a Woman.*

53. Merlin Stone. *When God was a Woman.*

54. Merlin Stone. *When God was a Woman* and Arthur George and Elena George. *The Mythology of Eden*

55. Carl Jung. "The Transcendent Function."

56. Clarissa Pinkola Estés. *Women Who Run with the Wolves: Myths and Stories of the Wild Woman Archetype.*

57. T.S. Eliot, *Four Quartets*

58. Clarissa Pinkola Estés. *Women Who Run with the Wolves: Myths and Stories of the Wild Woman Archetype.*

59. Mary Oliver. "When Death Comes."

60. James Hillman. *Thought of the Heart.*

61. James Hillman. *Thought of the Heart.*

62. Toko-pa Turner. *Belonging: Remembering Ourselves Home.*

63. adrienne marie brown. *Pleasure Activism: The Politics of Feeling Good.*

64. Mary Oliver. "Wild Geese."

65. Augustine. "Human Being."

66. John Phillips. *Eve: The History of an Idea.*

67. Toko-pa Turner. *Belonging: Remembering Ourselves Home.*

68. Thank you to Ursula Le Guin for teaching me about this relationship between emptiness and openness.

69. Robin Wall Kimmerer. *Braiding Sweetgrass: Indigenous Wisdom, Scientific Knowledge, and the Teaching of Plants.*

70. Andrew Fisher. *Radical Ecopsychology: Psychology in the Service of Life.*

71. Anne Baring and Jules Cashford. *Myth of the Goddess: Evolution of an Image.*

72. Carl Jung. *Modern Man in Search of Meaning.*

73. *Genesis* 3:6

74. *Genesis* 3: 17

75. David Abram. *Spell of the Sensuous.*

76. Carl Jung as cited by Meredith Sabini. *The Earth has a Soul: C.G. Jung on Nature, Technology and Modern Life.*

77. Beverly Lanzetta. *Radical Wisdom: A Feminist Mystical Theology.*

78. Thomas Moore. *The Care of The Soul: A Guide for Cultivating Depth and Sacredness in Everyday Life.*

79. James Hillman. *The Soul's Code: In Search of Character and Calling.*

80. See David Whyte's *Crossing the Unknown Sea: Work as a Pilgrimage of Identity* for more on elemental waters.

81. Clarissa Pinkola Estés. *Women Who Run with the Wolves: Myths and Stories of the Wild Woman Archetype.*

82. Susan Griffin. *Woman and Nature: The Roaring Inside Her.*

83. Carl Jung. *The Development of Personality.*

84. *Genesis* 3:15

85. Terry Tempest Williams. *When Women Were Birds.*

86. Tara Brach. *Radical Compassion: Learning to Love Yourself and Your World with the Practice of RAIN.*

87. Ursula Le Guin. *The Farthest Shore.*

88. For more on the transformation of the unconscious see Carl Jung's astounding book, *Answer to Job.*

89. May Sarton. *Journal of a Solitude.*

90. For more on this practice see Bill Plotkin's book *Soulcraft: Crossing into the Mysteries of Nature and Psyche.*

91. Marion Woodman and Elinor Dickson. *Dancing in the Flames: The Dark Goddess in the Transformation of Consciousness.*

92. James Hillman calls these theological wholeness and psychological wholeness.

93. Terry Tempest Williams. *When Women Were Birds.*

# ABOUT THE AUTHOR

Vanya Leilani is a depth psychologist, writer, teacher and storyteller. She has spent decades exploring the threshold where the external "shoulds" in our lives encounter our own wild knowing and un-knowing. She is passionate about helping us cultivate deeper friendship with our own lives as we learn to live from nature, rather than from obedience to the status quo and she devotes herself to this work through individual accompaniment, sacred gatherings, storytelling, teaching, and writing.

Vanya holds a PhD in Depth Psychology with emphasis in Jungian and Archetypal Studies. She has also completed a certificate training intensive with Dr Clarissa Pinkola Estés and has served as an adjunct professor at Pacifica Graduate Institute teaching on the creative power of archetypes.

Vanya was born and raised in southeastern Brazil and currently lives in the woods of the Pacific Northwest of the United States, where she tends to the land and many animals.

# ABOUT THE ARTIST

Natalia Berlik is an illustrator of children's books and an author of books about drawing from Poland. She has been illustrating professionally since 2017 and has written over 100 books for the most popular publishing houses in Poland.

Instagram @nb_ilustracje

behance.net/nataliaberlik

# ABOUT WOMANCRAFT

Womancraft Publishing was founded on the revolutionary vision that women and words can change the world. We act as midwife to transformational women's words that have the power to challenge, inspire, heal and speak to the silenced aspects of ourselves, empowering our readers to actively co-create cultures that value and support the female and feminine. Our books have been #1 Amazon bestsellers in many categories, as well as Nautilus and Women's Spirituality Award winners.

As we find ourselves in a time where old stories, old answers and ways of being are losing their authority and relevance, we at Womancraft are actively looking for new ways forward. Our books ask important questions. We aim to share a diverse range of voices, of different ages, backgrounds, sexual orientations and neurotypes, seeking every greater diversity, whilst acknowledging our limitations as a small press.

At the heart of our Womancraft philosophy is fairness and integrity. Creatives and women have always been underpaid: not on our watch! We split royalties 50:50 with our authors. We offer support and mentoring throughout the publishing process as standard. We use almost exclusively female artists on our covers, and as well as paying fairly for these cover images, offer a royalty share and promote the artists both in the books and online. Whilst far from perfect, we are proud that in our small way, Womancraft is walking its talk, living the new paradigm in the crumbling heart of the old: through financially empowering creative people, through words that honour the Feminine, through healthy working practices, and through integrating business with our lives, and rooting our economic decisions in what supports and sustains our natural environment. We are learning and improving all the time. I hope that one day soon, what we do is seen as nothing remarkable, just the norm.

We work on a full circle model of giving and receiving: reaching backwards, supporting Treesisters' reforestation projects and the UNHCR girls' education fund, and forwards via Worldreader, providing e-books at no-cost to education projects for girls and women in developing countries. We donate many paperback copies to education projects and women's libraries around the world. We speak from our place within the circle of women, sharing our vision, and encouraging them to share it onwards, in ever-widening circles.

We are honoured that the Womancraft community is growing internationally year on year, seeding red tents, book groups, women's circles, ceremonies and classes into the fabric of our world. Join the revolution! Sign up to the mailing list at womancraftpublishing.com and find us on social media for exclusive offers:

(f) womancraftpublishing

(○) womancraft_publishing

**Signed copies of all titles available from
shop.womancraftpublishing.com**

# Descent & Rising: Women's Stories & the Embodiment of the Inanna Myth

## Carly Mountain

*"The heroine is one who has remembered, reclaimed and reconnected with her unfettered red thread. She has been initiated into the spirit of the depths by her dark sister, and walks with newfound, embodied authority into the upperworld."*

What if, despite the uniqueness of your own life and experiences, each stage of the process of descent was universal? The journey of *Descent & Rising* is the core initiation of the feminine – the heroine's journey – one travelled by billions of women before you.

*Descent & Rising* explores real stories of women's descents into the underworld of the psyche – journeys of dissolution, grief and breakdown precipitated by trauma, fertility issues, loss of loved ones, mental health struggles, FGM, sexual abuse, birthing experiences, illness, war, burnout...

This is territory that Carly Mountain, psychotherapist and women's initiatory guide, knows intimately, and guides us through with exquisite care and insight, using the ancient Sumerian myth of the goddess Inanna as a blueprint. She maps not only the descent but the rising and familiarises us with a process of female psycho-spiritual growth overlooked in patriarchal culture.

*"The heroine's journey is an erotic, mystical initiation that revivifies our place in the shape of things... The fodder of our descents provides the compost from which the richest fruits of our lives can grow. If only we can turn towards our pain and let it work in us."*

## Muddy Mysticism: the Sacred Tethers of Body, Earth and Everyday

## Natalie Bryant Rizzieri

Like many women Natalie Bryant Rizzieri found the faith of her childhood no longer fitted…yet still there is a longing for the sacred. Through poetry, reflection and experience she moves into the possibility of direct experience with the divine…beyond a belief system. Exploring the possibility of daily life in the modern world not as something to be transcended or escaped…but as a mystical path in its own right.

*Muddy Mysticism* offers consolation to those who feel the truth and bewilderment that the late German Jesuit priest, Karl Rahner, touched upon when he said that the only way a person would survive with an intact faith in this century is by being a mystic.

Natalie Bryant-Rizzieri is an award-winning poet. This is her first non-fiction title.

## Walking with Persephone : A Journey of Midlife Descent and Renewal

## Molly Remer

Molly Remer invites us to take a walk with the goddess Persephone, whose story of descent into the Underworld has much to teach us. This book is a journey of soul-rebuilding, of putting the pieces of oneself back together.

*Walking with Persephone* weaves together personal insights and reflections with experiences in practical priestessing, family life, and explorations of the natural world. It advocates opening our eyes to the wonder around us, encouraging the reader to both look within themselves for truths about living, but also to the earth, the air, the animals, and plants we share our lives with.

Part memoir, part poetry, part soul guide, Molly's evocative voice is in the great American tradition of sacred nature writing.

# Crow Moon: reclaiming the wisdom of the dark woods

## Lucy H. Pearce

*"Suddenly the sky overhead is alive. From east and southeast, west and northwest, large black birds fly, travelling in their groups of hundreds are swirling, cawing, interweaving, dancing a greeting in the air. The sky is thick black feathered. We watch slack jawed as they combine and dissipate above our heads. Then, without signal or warning, they circle the heart of the wood and land in the trees, into hidden roosts, and silence falls once more."*

After months of feeling lost and burned out, a chance encounter with crows began an adventure in the dark woods – inner and outer – leading to a strange and powerful initiation.

Strikingly illustrated by the author, with contributions from over 30 women – artists, healers, authors – midlife women who have also been called by the strange magic of crows at decisive moments in their lives.

Enter the dark woods. Follow the crow, the moon and the mushroom on a journey of transformation and remembering.

# USE OF WOMANCRAFT WORK

Often women contact us asking if and how they may use our work. We love seeing our work out in the world. We love you sharing our words further. And we ask that you respect our hard work by acknowledging the source of the words.

We are delighted for short quotes from our books – up to 200 words – to be shared as memes or in your own articles or books, provided they are clearly accompanied by the author's name and the book's title.

We are also very happy for the materials in our books to be shared amongst women's communities: to be studied by book groups, discussed in classes, read from in ceremony, quoted on social media… with the following provisos:

☾ If content from the book is shared in written or spoken form, the book's author and title must be referenced clearly.

☾ The only person fully qualified to teach the material from any of our titles is the author of the book itself. There are no accredited teachers of this work. Please do not make claims of this sort.

☾ If you are creating a course devoted to the content of one of our books, its title and author must be clearly acknowledged on all promotional material (posters, websites, social media posts).

☾ The book's cover may be used in promotional materials or social media posts. The cover art is copyright of the artist and has been licensed exclusively for this book. Any element of the book's cover or font may not be used in branding your own marketing materials when teaching the content of the book, or content very similar to the original book.

☾ No more than two double page spreads, or four single pages of any book may be photocopied as teaching materials.

We are delighted to offer a 20% discount of over five copies going to one address. You can order these on our webshop, or email us.

If you require further clarification, email us at:
info@womancraftpublishing.com